Ladies' Home Journal

100 GREAT

COOKIE

RECIPES

LADIES' HOME JOURNAL™ BOOKS
New York/Des Moines

LADIES' HOME JOURNAL™ BOOKS
An Imprint of Meredith® Books

100 GREAT COOKIE RECIPES
Editor: Shelli McConnell
Writer/Researcher: Carol Prager
Copy Editor: Jennifer Miller
Associate Art Director: Tom Wegner
Food Stylist: Rick Ellis
Prop Stylist: Bette Blau
Photographer: Corinne Colen Photography
Cover Food Stylist: Janet Pittman
Cover Photographer: Mike Dieter
Electronic Production Coordinator: Paula Forest
Production Manager: Douglas Johnston

Vice President and Editorial Director: Elizabeth P. Rice
Executive Editor: Kay Sanders
Art Director: Ernest Shelton
Managing Editor: Christopher Cavanaugh

President, Book Group: Joseph J. Ward
Vice President, Retail Marketing: Jamie L. Martin
Vice President, Direct Marketing: Timothy Jarrell

On the cover: The Ultimate Chocolate Chunk Cookies (page 65)

LADIES' HOME JOURNAL®
Publishing Director and Editor-in-Chief: Myrna Blyth
Food Editor: Jan Turner Hazard
Associate Food Editors: Susan Sarao Westmoreland, Lisa Brainerd

Meredith Corporation
Chairman of the Executive Committee: E. T. Meredith III
Chairman of the Board, President and Chief Executive Officer: Jack D. Rehm
President and Chief Operating Officer: William T. Kerr

We Care!
All of us at Ladies' Home Journal™ Books are dedicated to providing you with the ideas and
recipe information you need to create wonderful foods. We welcome your comments and
suggestions. Write us at: Ladies' Home Journal™ Books, Cookbook Editorial Department,
RW-240, 1716 Locust St., Des Moines, IA 50309-3023.

If you would like to order additional copies of any of our books, call 1-800-678-2803.

To ensure that Ladies' Home Journal® recipes
meet the highest standards for flavor, nutrition,
appearance and reliability, we test them a
minimum of three times in our own kitchen.
That makes for quality you can count on.

Perfect Cookies

Cookies are a mouth-watering sweet that everyone loves to eat…and bake. Whether you stamp the dough into fanciful shapes, roll and slice it, or drop it from a teaspoon, making a batch of cookies is a satisfying, creative endeavor. Best of all, anytime can be cookie time! Perfect cookies have been a tradition at Ladies' Home Journal® for more than a century. So, we've got the recipes that let you bake your best, whether you're an expert cookie baker or an enthusiastic beginner.

CONTENTS

Classics from the Cookie Jar

A tried-and-true collection of treasured favorites.

All in the Pan

Quick to make and easy to bake—bar cookies.

Only Chocolate

Unbeatable fudgy morsels.

Heritage Traditions
Sweet specialties from the past, passed from one generation to the next.

Cookies for Christmas
Fit for the holiday, a fabulous array of festively decorated and heart-warming classic goodies.

Cookie Dazzlers
Truly spectacular, party-perfect delicacies.

Index

CLASSICS FROM

THE COOKIE JAR

This tried-and-true collection of homespun classics will win the appetites of children and adults alike. Who can resist snatching an extra Oatmeal-Raisin Cookie or a Cranberry-Lemon Iced Drop? Treat your family to a bit of old-fashioned goodness with our double delicious Gingery Gingersnaps or Snickerdoodles with a cinnamon-sugar coating. With a choice of so many perennially popular sweets, your only dilemma is which to bake first.

CRANBERRY-LEMON ICED DROPS

You get a double dose of lemon peel plus the zing of tart cranberries and toasted walnuts in these tangy cookies.

Prep time: 25 minutes
Baking time: 12 to 15 minutes per batch
O *Degree of difficulty: easy*

1½ cups chopped walnuts
1 cup all-purpose flour
1 teaspoon baking powder
½ teaspoon cinnamon
¼ teaspoon salt
½ cup butter *or* margarine, softened
½ cup granulated sugar
⅓ cup firmly packed brown sugar
¾ teaspoon grated lemon peel, divided
1 large egg
½ teaspoon vanilla extract
1½ cups cranberries, chopped
1 cup confectioners' sugar
2 tablespoons milk
   Pinch salt

1 Preheat oven to 350°F. Spread the walnuts on a baking sheet in a single layer. Bake 8 to 10 minutes, until lightly browned and fragrant. Cool. Leave the oven on.

2 Grease 2 cookie sheets. Combine the flour, baking powder, cinnamon, and salt in a medium bowl. Beat the butter, granulated sugar, brown sugar, and ½ teaspoon of the lemon peel in a large mixing bowl at medium speed until light and fluffy. Beat in the egg and vanilla. Beat in flour mixture at low speed just until combined. Stir in the walnuts and cranberries.

3 Drop dough by teaspoonfuls 2 inches apart onto prepared cookie sheets. Bake 12 to 15 minutes, until golden. Cool the cookies on cookie sheets 5 minutes, then transfer them to wire racks to cool completely.

4 For the icing, whisk together the confectioners' sugar, milk, the remaining ¼ teaspoon lemon peel, and a pinch of salt in a small bowl until smooth. Spread the icing over the tops of the cooled cookies. Let cookies stand until icing has set. Makes 4 dozen.

PER COOKIE		DAILY GOAL
Calories	80	2,000 (F), 2,500 (M)
Total Fat	5 g	60 g or less (F), 70 g or less (M)
Saturated fat	1 g	20 g or less (F), 23 g or less (M)
Cholesterol	10 mg	300 mg or less
Sodium	49 mg	2,400 mg or less
Carbohydrates	10 g	250 g or more
Protein	1 g	55 g to 90 g

NOTES

COCONUT CRISPS

We used simple tools to make these sweet treats so good looking: a glass to flatten cookies to an even thickness, and fork tines to make ridges.

Prep time: 10 minutes
Baking time: 10 to 12 minutes per batch
○ *Degree of difficulty: easy*
❋ *Can be frozen up to 3 months*

2 **cups all-purpose flour**
¾ **teaspoon baking powder**
¼ **teaspoon salt**
¾ **cup butter *or* margarine, softened**
1 **cup granulated sugar**
1 **large egg**
1 **teaspoon vanilla extract**
1½ **cups shredded sweetened coconut**

1 Preheat oven to 375°F. Combine the flour, baking powder, and salt in a medium bowl. Beat the butter and sugar in a large mixing bowl at medium speed until light and fluffy. Beat in the egg and vanilla. Beat in flour mixture at low speed just until combined. Stir in the coconut.

2 Drop dough by level tablespoonfuls onto ungreased cookie sheets. With the bottom of a glass dipped in flour, flatten each cookie to ¼-inch thickness, then lightly press with the tines of a fork to form ridges. Bake 10 to 12 minutes, until edges are golden. Transfer the cookies to wire racks to cool completely. Makes 3 dozen.

PER COOKIE		DAILY GOAL
Calories	100	2,000 (F), 2,500 (M)
Total Fat	5 g	60 g or less (F), 70 g or less (M)
Saturated fat	3 g	20 g or less (F), 23 g or less (M)
Cholesterol	16 mg	300 mg or less
Sodium	74 mg	2,400 mg or less
Carbohydrates	12 g	250 g or more
Protein	1 g	55 g to 90 g

OATMEAL-RAISIN COOKIES

If you like 'em soft and chewy, bake these classics until the edges are just golden. If you prefer your cookies crisp, bake them a couple of minutes more. *Also pictured on page 6.*

Prep time: 10 minutes
Baking time: 12 to 14 minutes per
   batch
Degree of difficulty: easy
Can be frozen up to 1 month

1	cup all-purpose flour
2	teaspoons baking soda
¾	teaspoon salt
¼	teaspoon nutmeg
½	cup butter *or* margarine, softened
1	cup firmly packed brown sugar
½	cup granulated sugar
1	teaspoon vanilla extract
2	large eggs
3	cups old-fashioned oats, uncooked
1½	cups raisins

1 Preheat oven to 350°F. Grease 2 cookie sheets. Combine the flour, baking soda, salt, and nutmeg in a medium bowl. Beat the butter, brown sugar, and granulated sugar in a large mixing bowl at medium speed until light and fluffy. Stir in the vanilla. Add the eggs, one at a time, beating well after each addition. Beat in the flour mixture at low speed just until combined. Stir in the oats and raisins.

2 Drop dough by heaping tablespoonfuls 2 inches apart onto the prepared cookie sheets. Bake 12 to 14 minutes, until the tops are golden. Cool the cookies on cookie sheets 1 minute, then transfer them to wire racks to cool completely. Makes 2½ dozen.

PER COOKIE		DAILY GOAL
Calories	140	2,000 (F), 2,500 (M)
Total Fat	4 g	60 g or less (F), 70 g or less (M)
Saturated fat	2 g	20 g or less (F), 23 g or less (M)
Cholesterol	22 mg	300 mg or less
Sodium	180 mg	2,400 mg or less
Carbohydrates	25 g	250 g or more
Protein	2 g	55 g to 90 g

NOTES

11

BENNE WAFERS

This famous wafer-thin cookie from the old South features "benne" or sesame seeds. You'll love the toasted nutty flavor of these delicate treats.

Prep time: 15 minutes
Baking time: 5 to 7 minutes per batch
O *Degree of difficulty: easy*
❄ *Can be frozen up to 3 months*

1 cup all-purpose flour
¼ teaspoon baking powder
¼ teaspoon salt
½ cup butter *or* margarine, softened
1 cup firmly packed light brown
    sugar
1 large egg
2 tablespoons water
1 teaspoon vanilla extract
¼ cup sesame (benne) seeds

1 Preheat oven to 375°F. Grease 2 cookie sheets. Sift the flour, baking powder, and salt onto a sheet of wax paper. Beat the butter and brown sugar in a large mixing bowl at medium speed until light. Add the egg, water, and vanilla and beat until light and fluffy. Beat in flour mixture at low speed just until combined. Stir in the sesame seeds.

2 Drop dough by level teaspoonfuls 2 inches apart onto prepared cookie sheets. Bake 5 to 7 minutes, until the edges are golden. Transfer the cookies to wire racks to cool completely. Makes 8 dozen.

PER COOKIE		DAILY GOAL
Calories	25	2,000 (F), 2,500 (M)
Total Fat	1 g	60 g or less (F), 70 g or less (M)
Saturated fat	1 g	20 g or less (F), 23 g or less (M)
Cholesterol	5 mg	300 mg or less
Sodium	19 mg	2,400 mg or less
Carbohydrates	3 g	250 g or more
Protein	0 g	55 g to 90 g

DELUXE COCONUT-OATMEAL COOKIES

These extra-large cookies are pure indulgence and are especially good served with vanilla ice cream.

Prep time: 15 minutes
Baking time: 12 to 15 minutes
◯ *Degree of difficulty: easy*
❄ *Can be frozen up to 3 months*

1	cup shredded sweetened coconut
2	cups all-purpose flour
1	teaspoon baking powder
¾	teaspoon cinnamon
½	teaspoon baking soda
½	teaspoon salt
¼	teaspoon allspice
1	cup butter *or* margarine, softened
1¼	cups firmly packed brown sugar
2	large eggs
1	teaspoon vanilla extract
1½	cups old-fashioned oats, uncooked

1 Preheat oven to 350°F. Spread the coconut on a baking sheet in a single layer. Bake 6 to 8 minutes, until lightly toasted and fragrant. Cool. Leave oven on.

2 Grease 2 cookie sheets. Combine the flour, baking powder, cinnamon, baking soda, salt, and allspice in a medium bowl. Beat the butter and brown sugar in a large mixing bowl at medium speed until light and fluffy. Add the eggs, one at a time, beating well after each addition. Beat in the vanilla. Beat in flour mixture at low speed just until combined. Stir in the toasted coconut and the oats.

3 For each cookie, drop 2 rounded tablespoonfuls of dough together, 2 inches apart onto prepared cookie sheets. Bake 12 to 15 minutes, until the tops are golden. Cool the cookies on cookie sheets 5 minutes, then transfer them to wire racks to cool completely. Makes 20 cookies.

PER COOKIE		DAILY GOAL
Calories	230	2,000 (F), 2,500 (M)
Total Fat	12 g	60 g or less (F), 70 g or less (M)
Saturated fat	7 g	20 g or less (F), 23 g or less (M)
Cholesterol	46 mg	300 mg or less
Sodium	230 mg	2,400 mg or less
Carbohydrates	29 g	250 g or more
Protein	3 g	55 g to 90 g

HERMITS

This molasses drop cookie filled with dried fruits and nuts can be traced back to Colonial times. To make them even more irresistible, we've topped these spicy nuggets with creamy vanilla frosting.

Prep time: 20 minutes
Baking time: 13 to 15 minutes per batch
O *Degree of difficulty: easy*

- 3 **cups all-purpose flour**
- 1 **teaspoon baking soda**
- 1 **teaspoon cinnamon**
- ½ **teaspoon nutmeg**
- ¼ **teaspoon cloves**
- ¼ **teaspoon salt**
- ¾ **cup vegetable shortening**
- 1 **cup firmly packed brown sugar**
- ½ **cup light molasses**
- 2 **large eggs**
- ½ **cup sour cream**
- 1 **cup raisins**
- 1 **cup chopped dried figs**
- 1 **cup chopped walnuts**

- ¼ **cup butter** *or* **margarine, softened**
- 2 **cups confectioners' sugar**
- 1 **teaspoon vanilla extract**
- 3 **to 4 tablespoons milk**

1 Preheat oven to 350°F. Combine the flour, baking soda, cinnamon, nutmeg, cloves, and salt in a medium bowl. Beat the shortening and brown sugar in a large mixing bowl at medium speed until light and fluffy. Beat in the molasses, eggs, and sour cream. Beat in flour mixture at low speed just until combined. Stir in the raisins, figs, and walnuts.

2 Drop dough by rounded teaspoonfuls 1½ inches apart onto ungreased cookie sheets. Bake 13 to 15 minutes, until golden. Transfer the cookies to wire racks to cool completely.

3 For frosting, beat the butter and confectioners' sugar in a mixing bowl until combined; add vanilla. Beat in the milk, one tablespoon at a time, until frosting is smooth and spreadable. Spread frosting over the cooled cookies. Let cookies stand until frosting sets. Makes 7 dozen.

PER COOKIE		DAILY GOAL
Calories	90	2,000 (F), 2,500 (M)
Total Fat	4 g	60 g or less (F), 70 g or less (M)
Saturated fat	1 g	20 g or less (F), 23 g or less (M)
Cholesterol	7 mg	300 mg or less
Sodium	32 mg	2,400 mg or less
Carbohydrates	13 g	250 g or more
Protein	1 g	55 g to 90 g

NOTES

GRANOLA DROPS

Here's a low-fat, high-fiber treat from the cookie jar. Try them for breakfast with a glass of orange juice.

▼ *Low-fat*
  Prep time: 20 minutes
  Baking time: 15 minutes
○ *Degree of difficulty: easy*

½ **cup all-purpose flour**
¼ **teaspoon baking soda**
¼ **teaspoon salt**
¼ **cup vegetable oil**
½ **cup firmly packed brown sugar**
¼ **cup honey**
2 **tablespoons water**
1½ **cups old-fashioned oats, uncooked**
½ **cup chopped dried figs**
½ **cup chopped dried pears** *or* **apple slices**
¼ **cup sliced natural almonds**

1 Preheat oven to 350°F. Grease 2 cookie sheets. Combine the flour, baking soda, and salt in a small bowl. Whisk together the oil, brown sugar, honey, and water in a large bowl until smooth. Gradually add flour mixture to oil-sugar mixture until well combined. Stir in the oats, figs, pears and almonds.

2 Drop dough by tablespoonfuls onto prepared cookie sheets. Bake 15 minutes, rotating the cookie sheets halfway through. Transfer the cookies to wire racks to cool completely. Makes 2 dozen.

PER COOKIE		DAILY GOAL
Calories	105	2,000 (F), 2,500 (M)
Total Fat	3 g	60 g or less (F), 70 g or less (M)
Saturated fat	1 g	20 g or less (F), 23 g or less (M)
Cholesterol	0 mg	300 mg or less
Sodium	42 mg	2,400 mg or less
Carbohydrates	18 g	250 g or more
Protein	1 g	55 g to 90 g

15

SNICKERDOODLES

These chewy cinnamon cookies were called schneckenoodles in the cookbooks of 19th-century German and Dutch settlers.

Prep time: 10 minutes plus chilling
Baking time: 12 to 14 minutes per batch
Degree of difficulty: easy
Can be frozen up to 1 month

2¾ **cups all-purpose flour**
  2 **teaspoons cream of tartar**
  1 **teaspoon baking soda**
 ¼ **teaspoon salt**
  1 **cup butter *or* margarine, softened**
1¾ **cups granulated sugar, divided**
  2 **large eggs**
  4 **teaspoons cinnamon**

1 Combine the flour, cream of tartar, baking soda, and salt in a medium bowl. Beat the butter, 1½ cups of the sugar, and the eggs in a large mixing bowl at medium speed until light and fluffy. Beat in flour mixture at low speed until well combined. Cover and refrigerate dough 1 hour.

2 Preheat oven to 375°F. Combine remaining ¼ cup sugar and the cinnamon in a shallow bowl. Shape chilled dough into 1-inch balls and roll them in the cinnamon-sugar mixture. Place the balls 3 inches apart on ungreased cookie sheets. Bake 12 to 14 minutes, until golden brown. Transfer the cookies to a wire rack to cool completely. Makes 4½ dozen.

PER COOKIE		DAILY GOAL
Calories	80	2,000 (F), 2,500 (M)
Total Fat	4 g	60 g or less (F), 70 g or less (M)
Saturated fat	2 g	20 g or less (F), 23 g or less (M)
Cholesterol	17 mg	300 mg or less
Sodium	71 mg	2,400 mg or less
Carbohydrates	11 g	250 g or more
Protein	1 g	55 g to 90 g

NOTES

FILBERTINES

Hazelnut lovers of the world, this is the cookie for you. A touch of ground cardamom makes this shaped cookie extra special.

Prep time: 15 minutes plus chilling
Baking time: 15 minutes per batch
O *Degree of difficulty: easy*
❋ *Can be frozen up to 3 months*

½ **cup chopped hazelnuts**
1⅓ **cups all-purpose flour**
½ **teaspoon baking soda**
⅛ **teaspoon cardamom**
½ **cup butter *or* margarine, softened**
½ **cup granulated sugar**
1 **large egg**
30 **whole hazelnuts**

1 Preheat oven to 350°F. Spread the hazelnuts on a baking sheet in a single layer. Bake 8 to 10 minutes, until lightly browned. Turn off oven.

2 Combine the flour, baking soda, and cardamom in a medium bowl. Beat the butter and sugar in a large mixing bowl at medium speed until light. Beat in the egg until light and fluffy. Beat in flour mixture at low speed until combined. Cover and refrigerate 1 hour, until dough is firm.

3 Preheat oven to 350°F. Grease 2 cookie sheets. Spread chopped hazelnuts on a plate. Shape chilled dough into 1-inch balls and roll in chopped nuts. Place the balls 2 inches apart on prepared cookie sheets. Lightly press a whole hazelnut into the center of each cookie. Bake 15 minutes, until lightly browned and firm. Transfer the cookies to wire racks to cool completely. Makes about 30 cookies.

PER COOKIE		DAILY GOAL
Calories	90	2,000 (F), 2,500 (M)
Total Fat	6 g	60 g or less (F), 70 g or less (M)
Saturated fat	2 g	20 g or less (F), 23 g or less (M)
Cholesterol	16 mg	300 mg or less
Sodium	61 mg	2,400 mg or less
Carbohydrates	9 g	250 g or more
Protein	1 g	55 g to 90 g

NOTES

GINGERY GINGERSNAPS

A double delicious whammy of fresh and ground ginger spices up this cookie jar favorite.

Prep time: 15 minutes plus chilling
Baking time: 8 to 9 minutes per batch
O *Degree of difficulty: easy*
❄ *Can be frozen up to 3 months*

2¼ cups all-purpose flour
1½ teaspoons baking soda
1 teaspoon ground ginger
½ teaspoon cinnamon
½ teaspoon salt
⅛ teaspoon cloves
1 cup butter *or* margarine, softened
1½ cups granulated sugar, divided
¼ cup light molasses
1 large egg
1 tablespoon grated fresh ginger
1 teaspoon vanilla extract

1 Combine the flour, baking soda, ground ginger, cinnamon, salt, and cloves in a medium bowl. Beat the butter and 1 cup of the sugar in a large mixing bowl at medium speed until light and fluffy. Beat in the molasses, then the egg, grated ginger, and vanilla. Beat in flour mixture at low speed just until combined. Refrigerate 1 hour, until dough is very firm.

2 Preheat oven to 375°F. Grease 2 cookie sheets. Shape chilled dough into 1-inch balls and roll them in the remaining ½ cup sugar. Place the balls 2 inches apart on prepared cookie sheets. Bake 8 to 9 minutes, until just firm *(do not overbake)*. Transfer the cookies to wire racks to cool completely. Makes 3½ dozen.

PER COOKIE		DAILY GOAL
Calories	100	2,000 (F), 2,500 (M)
Total Fat	5 g	60 g or less (F), 70 g or less (M)
Saturated fat	3 g	20 g or less (F), 23 g or less (M)
Cholesterol	17 mg	300 mg or less
Sodium	120 mg	2,400 mg or less
Carbohydrates	14 g	250 g or more
Protein	1 g	55 g to 90 g

19

WALNUT THUMBPRINTS

Try filling these pretty cookie buttons with an assortment of brightly colored preserves.

Prep time: 20 minutes
Baking time: 10 to 12 minutes per batch
○ *Degree of difficulty: easy*
❋ *Can be frozen up to 3 months*

1½ **cups coarsely chopped walnuts**
1 **cup butter, softened (no substitutions)**
¾ **cup granulated sugar**
2¼ **cups all-purpose flour**
¼ **cup seedless raspberry jam *or* other jams**
   Confectioners' sugar

1 Preheat oven to 350°F. Chop the walnuts in a food processor until very fine. Beat the butter and granulated sugar in a large mixing bowl at medium speed until light and fluffy. Beat in chopped walnuts. Beat in the flour at low speed just until combined.

2 Shape dough into 1-inch balls. Place the balls 2 inches apart on ungreased cookie sheets. Flatten each ball with the bottom of a glass to a 1½-inch circle. Press a ½-inch indentation into the center of each cookie with your fingertip or the handle of a wooden spoon. Fill each indentation with ¼ teaspoon of preserves. Bake 10 to 12 minutes, until golden. Transfer the cookies to wire racks to cool completely. Sift confectioners' sugar over cookies. Makes 6 dozen.

PER COOKIE		DAILY GOAL
Calories	65	2,000 (F), 2,500 (M)
Total Fat	4 g	60 g or less (F), 70 g or less (M)
Saturated fat	2 g	20 g or less (F), 23 g or less (M)
Cholesterol	7 mg	300 mg or less
Sodium	27 mg	2,400 mg or less
Carbohydrates	7 g	250 g or more
Protein	1 g	55 g to 90 g

CLASSIC PEANUT BUTTER COOKIES

Kids of all ages will love making these chewy, sugar-coated members of the Cookie Hall-of-Fame, then devouring them with plenty of ice-cold milk.

Prep time: 30 minutes
Baking time: 8 to 10 minutes per batch
O *Degree of difficulty: easy*
❋ *Can be frozen up to 3 months*

2½ cups all-purpose flour
1½ teaspoons baking soda
1 teaspoon baking powder
¼ teaspoon salt
1 cup butter *or* margarine, softened
1 cup peanut butter
1 cup firmly packed brown sugar
1⅓ cups granulated sugar, divided
2 large eggs
1 teaspoon vanilla extract

1 Preheat oven to 375°F. Combine the flour, baking soda, baking powder, and salt in a medium bowl. Beat the butter, peanut butter, brown sugar, and 1 cup of the granulated sugar in a large mixing bowl at medium speed until light and fluffy. Beat in the eggs and vanilla. Beat in flour mixture at low speed just until combined.

2 Shape dough into 1-inch balls and roll them in the remaining ⅓ cup granulated sugar. Place the balls 2 inches apart on 2 ungreased cookie sheets. With sugar-coated fork tines, press and flatten each ball, making a criss-cross pattern. Bake 8 to 10 minutes, until golden. Cool the cookies on cookie sheets 5 minutes, then transfer them to wire racks to cool completely. Makes 6 dozen.

PER COOKIE		DAILY GOAL
Calories	90	2,000 (F), 2,500 (M)
Total Fat	4 g	60 g or less (F), 70 g or less (M)
Saturated fat	2 g	20 g or less (F), 23 g or less (M)
Cholesterol	13 mg	300 mg or less
Sodium	86 mg	2,400 mg or less
Carbohydrates	10 g	250 g or more
Protein	2 g	55 g to 90 g

A BAKER'S DOZEN TECHNIQUE TIPS!

1. Read the recipe carefully and gather all your ingredients before getting started.

2. Measure all ingredients accurately. Use nested metal cups and measuring spoons to measure flour and other dry ingredients. Measure liquids in clear measuring cups with spouts. To accurately read, hold the cup at eye level.

3. All recipes were tested with both stand and portable mixers. Beating the butter and sugar at medium or medium-high speed and dry ingredients at low speed. When adding the dry ingredients, beat just until combined.

4. Use a minimum of 2 large, heavy-duty cookie sheets. For proper air circulation, cookie sheets should not have rims. The heavier the baking sheet, the more evenly the heat will be distributed. Thinner cookie sheets may cause cookies to bake too quickly and burn.

5. For easy greasing of cookie sheets, use vegetable cooking spray or solid vegetable shortening. Butter is more likely to burn, and its moisture content can cause the cookies to stick.

6. For even baking, make your cookies uniform in size and thickness. For dropped and rolled cookies, arrange in neat, even rows 2 or 3 inches apart on prepared cookie sheets.

7. When heating the oven, always allow 15 minutes for your oven to reach the proper temperature. Because oven temperatures can vary greatly, place an oven thermometer in the center of your oven rack. Have the oven gauge adjusted if the temperature varies more than 25 degrees from your setting.

8. For best results, bake one sheet of cookies at a time on the center rack of your oven. If you wish to bake 2 sheets of cookies, place on two evenly spaced oven racks, one in the top third of the oven, the other in the bottom third. Remember that the cookies on the top rack will brown more quickly, so halfway through baking, rotate pans from one rack to the other.

9. Use a timer. Check cookies for doneness at the minimum baking time.

Some cookies may be ready and need to be removed; others can bake longer if necessary.

10. Unless otherwise noted, immediately transfer hot cookies with a metal spatula to wire racks to cool completely. Cool the cookies in a single layer on the racks.

11. Always allow baking sheets to cool between batches of cookies. A hot baking sheet will cause cookies to spread and bake unevenly.

12. Cool cookies completely before storing. Most cookies keep well if placed in air-tight containers and stored at room temperature for a few days.

13. For longer storage, cookies should be frozen. To freeze, cool cookies completely, then place cookies between sheets of wax paper in airtight, freezer-proof containers. (Recipes marked with an asterisk and number denote cookies that can be frozen and for how many months.) To thaw only some of the cookies, place them in a single layer on a serving plate for about 15 minutes.

ALMOND MACAROONS

These chewy cookies have all the old-fashioned sugar and almond flavor you could ask for, but no cholesterol.

Prep time: 20 minutes
Baking time: 13 to 15 minutes per batch
⬤ *Degree of difficulty: moderate*

1   tube (7 ounces) *or* 1 can (8 ounces) almond paste
¾   cup granulated sugar
⅓   cup confectioners' sugar
2   large egg whites
    Confectioners' sugar

1 Preheat oven to 325°F. Line 2 cookie sheets with foil, then grease and flour the foil. Beat the almond paste, granulated sugar, and the ⅓ cup confectioners' sugar in a large mixing bowl at low speed until the mixture resembles coarse crumbs. With mixer at medium speed, beat in the egg whites, one at a time, until smooth.

2 Spoon dough into a large pastry bag fitted with a ½-inch plain tip. Pipe ¾-inch rounds 1½ inches apart on prepared cookie sheets. Sift with confectioners' sugar.

3 Bake 13 to 15 minutes, rotating the cookie sheets halfway through, until the cookies are golden. Transfer the foil to wire racks to cool cookies completely. Carefully peel the cooled cookies from foil. Makes 4½ dozen.

PER COOKIE		DAILY GOAL
Calories	35	2,000 (F), 2,500 (M)
Total Fat	1 g	60 g or less (F), 70 g or less (M)
Saturated fat	0 g	20 g or less (F), 23 g or less (M)
Cholesterol	0 mg	300 mg or less
Sodium	4 mg	2,400 mg or less
Carbohydrates	6 g	250 g or more
Protein	1 g	55 g to 90 g

BUTTERSCOTCH ICEBOX COOKIES

You don't need to bake all these cookies at once. Just keep some of the dough in your freezer and bake a batch of buttery wafers at a moment's notice.

Prep time: 15 minutes plus chilling
Baking time: 12 to 15 minutes per batch
Degree of difficulty: easy
Can be frozen up to 3 months

2 **cups all-purpose flour**
½ **teaspoon baking powder**
½ **teaspoon salt**
¾ **cup butter** *or* **margarine, softened**
¾ **cup firmly packed dark brown sugar**
1 **large egg**
1 **teaspoon vanilla extract**
1 **cup chopped pecans** *or* **walnuts**

1 Combine the flour, baking powder, and salt in a medium bowl. Beat the butter and brown sugar in a large mixing bowl at medium speed until light and fluffy. Beat in the egg and vanilla. Beat in flour mixture at low speed just until combined. Stir in the pecans. Shape dough into a 6x3x2-inch brick. Wrap the brick in wax paper and freeze dough at least 2 hours or refrigerate at least 6 hours or overnight, until very firm.

2 Preheat oven to 350°F. With a long sharp knife, cut the dough into ⅛-inch-thick slices. Place the slices 1 inch apart on ungreased cookie sheets. Bake 12 to 15 minutes, until edges are lightly browned. Transfer the cookies to wire racks to cool completely. Makes 2 dozen.

PER COOKIE		DAILY GOAL
Calories	150	2,000 (F), 2,500 (M)
Total Fat	9 g	60 g or less (F), 70 g or less (M)
Saturated fat	4 g	20 g or less (F), 23 g or less (M)
Cholesterol	24 mg	300 mg or less
Sodium	120 mg	2,400 mg or less
Carbohydrates	16 g	250 g or more
Protein	2 g	55 g to 90 g

STRAIGHT FROM THE ICEBOX

Super convenient, icebox cookies can be prepared well in advance. Prepared dough is ready to slice and bake at a moments notice. Unbaked logs may be refrigerated up to 3 days or frozen up to 3 months.

To shape dough into a log, transfer dough with a rubber spatula to a sheet of waxed paper or plastic wrap. (If the recipe calls for two logs, divide the dough in half and place on 2 sheets of waxed paper.) Using the waxed paper as a guide, lift and roll the dough to the dimensions given in the recipe. Refrigerate or freeze the dough as directed. When the dough is firm, slice and bake just a portion of the dough, or the entire log.

LEMON-CORNMEAL WAFERS

Here's a dressed-up basic cookie for the cookie jar complete with tart lemon icing and a candied lemon-peel garnish.

Prep time: 35 minutes plus chilling
Baking time: 10 to 12 minutes per batch
Degree of difficulty: moderate
❄ *Can be frozen up to 3 months*

1½ **cups all-purpose flour**
1 **cup yellow cornmeal**
1 **cup unsalted butter, softened**
    (no substitutions)
1¼ **cups granulated sugar, divided**
2 **large egg yolks**
1 **teaspoon grated lemon peel**
1 **whole lemon**
¼ **cup water**
3 **to 5 teaspoons fresh lemon juice**
1 **cup confectioners' sugar**

1 Combine the flour and cornmeal in a medium bowl. Beat the butter and ¾ cup of the granulated sugar in a large mixing bowl at medium speed until light and fluffy. Add the egg yolks and lemon peel and beat until well blended. Beat in flour mixture at low speed just until combined. Divide dough in half. Shape each half into a 10-inch-long log. Wrap the logs in wax paper and refrigerate 4 hours or overnight.

2 Preheat oven to 350°F. Cut logs into ¼-inch-thick slices. Place the slices 1 inch apart on ungreased cookie sheets. Bake 10 to 12 minutes, until firm. Transfer the cookies to wire racks to cool completely.

3 With a swivel-blade peeler, remove the peel from the whole lemon and cut it into 1½-inch long strips. Combine ¼ cup of the granulated sugar and water in a small saucepan. Bring to a boil; add the lemon peel and cook 5 minutes. Drain and cool the peel on paper towels. Toss the strips with the remaining ¼ cup granulated sugar.

4 For glaze, stir 3 teaspoons of the lemon juice into the confectioners' sugar to make a smooth glaze. Add more juice if needed to make the glaze spreadable.

5 Spread each cookie with the lemon glaze and garnish with the candied lemon peel. Let the cookies stand until glaze is set. Makes 6 dozen.

PER COOKIE		DAILY GOAL
Calories	60	2,000 (F), 2,500 (M)
Total Fat	3 g	60 g or less (F), 70 g or less (M)
Saturated fat	2 g	20 g or less (F), 23 g or less (M)
Cholesterol	13 mg	300 mg or less
Sodium	1 mg	2,400 mg or less
Carbohydrates	8 g	250 g or more
Protein	1 g	55 g to 90 g

NOTES

OLD-FASHIONED SOUR CREAM COOKIES

It's easy to imagine grandma stocking her cookie jar to the brim with these tender sugar cookies.

Prep time: 30 minutes
Baking time: 8 to 10 minutes per batch
◖ *Degree of difficulty: moderate*
❋ *Can be frozen up to 3 months*

2⅔ **cups all-purpose flour**
1 **teaspoon baking powder**
½ **teaspoon baking soda**
½ **teaspoon salt**
¼ **teaspoon nutmeg**
½ **cup butter, softened (no substitutions)**
1 **cup granulated sugar**
1 **large egg**
1 **teaspoon vanilla extract**
½ **cup sour cream**
  Granulated sugar

1 Preheat oven to 375°F. Grease 2 cookie sheets. Combine the flour, baking powder, baking soda, salt, and nutmeg in a medium bowl. Beat the butter, the 1 cup sugar, egg, and vanilla in a large mixing bowl at medium speed until light and fluffy. Beat in flour mixture alternately with the sour cream, at low speed, beginning and ending with flour mixture, just until combined.

2 Divide dough in half. On a sheet of floured wax paper, roll one dough half ¼-inch thick. Cut the dough with floured, 2-inch cookie cutters into desired shapes. Place the cookies 2 inches apart on prepared cookie sheets. Sprinkle the tops of cookies with additional sugar. Bake 8 to 10 minutes, until lightly browned. Transfer the cookies to wire racks to cool completely. Repeat rolling and cutting remaining dough, rerolling the scraps. Makes 5 dozen.

PER COOKIE		DAILY GOAL
Calories	55	2,000 (F), 2,500 (M)
Total Fat	4 g	60 g or less (F), 70 g or less (M)
Saturated fat	1 g	20 g or less (F), 23 g or less (M)
Cholesterol	9 mg	300 mg or less
Sodium	37 mg	2,400 mg or less
Carbohydrates	13 g	250 g or more
Protein	2 g	55 g to 90 g

OE FROGGERS

According to legend, these molasses-rum cookies were created by a New Englander named Old Joe, who lived by a frog pond. Big and chewy, the flavor of these cut-outs only improves when they are stored in an air-tight cookie jar.

Prep time: 30 minutes plus chilling
Baking time: 8 to 12 minutes per
*   batch*
Degree of difficulty: moderate
Can be frozen up to 3 months

4½   **cups all-purpose flour**
1½   **teaspoons salt**
1½   **teaspoons ginger**
½   **teaspoon cloves**
½   **teaspoon allspice**
½   **teaspoon nutmeg**
½   **cup butter** *or* **margarine, softened**
1   **cup granulated sugar**
1   **cup light molasses**
1   **teaspoon baking soda**
⅓   **cup dark rum**
3   **tablespoons hot water**

1   Combine the flour, salt, ginger, cloves, allspice, and nutmeg in a large bowl. Beat the butter and sugar in a large mixing bowl at medium speed until light and fluffy. Gradually beat in flour mixture at low speed just until combined. Combine the molasses and baking soda in a small bowl, then add to the dough and beat well. Combine the rum and hot water; pour into the mixture and beat at low speed until well mixed. Wrap dough in wax paper and refrigerate 2 hours or overnight.

2   Preheat oven to 375°F. Grease 2 cookie sheets. Divide dough into quarters. On a pastry cloth or well-floured surface, roll one dough portion to a scant ¼-inch thickness (keep remaining dough refrigerated). Cut the dough with a floured, 4-inch round or decorative cookie cutter. Transfer the cut-outs to prepared cookie sheets. Bake 10 to 12 minutes, until edges are set. Transfer the cookies to wire racks to cool completely. Repeat rolling and cutting remaining dough, rerolling the scraps. Makes 3½ dozen.

PER COOKIE		DAILY GOAL
Calories	115	2,000 (F), 2,500 (M)
Total Fat	2.5 g	60 g or less (F), 70 g or less (M)
Saturated fat	1 g	20 g or less (F), 23 g or less (M)
Cholesterol	6 mg	300 mg or less
Sodium	136 mg	2,400 mg or less
Carbohydrates	20 g	250 g or more
Protein	1 g	55 g to 90 g

NOTES

ALL IN

THE PAN

Mix up a batch of cookie dough, then pour it in a pan and bake. It's quick! It's easy! It's bar cookies! And, we've selected our most scrumptious recipes. Try our creamy Raspberry Cheesecake Bars or the almond-filled Apricot Frangipane Bars. Where are the brownies? We offer you a choice selection of All-American favorites. These simply sweet temptations are the best you've ever tasted...

bar none!

APRICOT FRANGIPANE BARS

This elegant bar cookie features a unique layer of puréed dried apricots, which lends subtle, tart contrast to the sweet almond filling.

Prep time: 30 minutes plus cooling
Baking time: 30 to 35 minutes
● *Degree of difficulty: moderate*
❄ *Can be frozen up to 3 months*

2½ cups water
2 cups (12 ounces) dried apricots
1 cup granulated sugar, divided
2¼ cups all-purpose flour
⅛ teaspoon salt
½ cup chilled butter, cut up
    (no substitutions)
¼ cup vegetable shortening
3 to 4 tablespoons ice water

Almond Topping
1 cup granulated sugar
1 tube (7 ounces) *or* 1 can (8 ounces)
    almond paste
¾ cup butter, softened
    (no substitutions)

4 large eggs
½ cup all-purpose flour
1 teaspoon vanilla extract
½ teaspoon almond extract
⅛ teaspoon salt
    Confectioners' sugar

1 For the apricot filling, bring the water, apricots, and ¾ cup of the sugar to a boil in a small saucepan. Reduce heat and simmer until the apricots are tender, about 20 minutes. Remove from heat and mash with a fork until smooth. Cool completely.

2 Preheat oven to 400°F. Meanwhile, for the crust, combine the flour, the remaining ¼ cup sugar, and salt in a medium bowl. With a pastry blender or 2 knives, cut in the butter and shortening until the mixture resembles coarse crumbs. Sprinkle it with ice water, 1 tablespoon at a time, tossing with a fork until mixture is moist enough to hold together. Roll pastry into a 15½x10½-inch rectangle and place in a same-size jelly-roll pan. Bake 15 to 17 minutes, until golden brown. Cool the crust completely in the pan on a wire rack.

3 For the Almond Topping, beat the sugar, almond paste, and butter in a large mixing bowl at medium speed until light and fluffy. Add the eggs, one at a time, beating well after each addition. Beat in the flour, vanilla, almond extract, and salt at low speed until smooth.

4 Reduce oven temperature to 350°F. Spread the apricot filling evenly over the baked crust. Top the crust evenly with the almond mixture. Bake 30 to 35 minutes, until toothpick inserted in center comes out clean. Cool completely in the pan on a wire rack. Cut into 3x1-inch bars. Sprinkle with confectioners' sugar. Makes 50.

PER COOKIE		DAILY GOAL
Calories	150	2,000 (F), 2,500 (M)
Total Fat	7 g	60 g or less (F), 70 g or less (M)
Saturated fat	3 g	20 g or less (F), 23 g or less (M)
Cholesterol	29 mg	300 mg or less
Sodium	64 mg	2,400 mg or less
Carbohydrates	20 g	250 g or more
Protein	2 g	55 g to 90 g

NOTES

WHOLE WHEAT-RAISIN BARS

Grinding the walnuts and raisins is the key to giving these bars a cakelike texture.

Prep time: 15 minutes plus cooling
Baking time: 35 to 40 minutes
Degree of difficulty: easy

1   cup raisins
1   cup walnuts
1   cup hot water
1   teaspoon baking soda
½   cups whole wheat flour
½   cups all-purpose flour
1   teaspoon cinnamon
½   teaspoon nutmeg
½   teaspoon baking powder
1   cup butter *or* margarine, softened
½   cups firmly packed brown sugar
2   large eggs
1   teaspoon vanilla extract
½   cup chopped walnuts

1 Preheat oven to 350°F. Grease and flour a 15½x10½-inch jelly-roll pan. Combine the raisin and walnuts and put them through a food grinder. Combine the hot water and baking soda in a small bowl, then stir in the raisin-walnut mixture. Combine the whole wheat flour, all-purpose flour, cinnamon, nutmeg, and baking powder in a medium bowl.

2 Beat the butter and brown sugar in a large mixing bowl until light and fluffy. Add the eggs, one at a time, beating well after each addition. Beat in the vanilla. Add the flour mixture alternately with raisin-walnut mixture, beating at low speed, beginning and ending with flour. Stir in the chopped walnuts. Spread batter in the prepared pan. Bake 35 to 40 minutes. Cool completely in the pan on a wire rack. Cut into 2½x1½-inch bars. Makes 42.

PER COOKIE		DAILY GOAL
Calories	140	2,000 (F), 2,500 (M)
Total Fat	7 g	60 g or less (F), 70 g or less (M)
Saturated fat	3 g	20 g or less (F), 23 g or less (M)
Cholesterol	22 mg	300 mg or less
Sodium	76 mg	2,400 mg or less
Carbohydrates	18 g	250 g or more
Protein	2 g	55 g to 90 g

33

RASPBERRY CHEESECAKE BARS

These triple-layer cookie fingers feature a nutty crumb crust, luscious raspberry jam, and a creamy cheesecake filling. Wonderful for a crowd, these bars can be prepared up to 2 days ahead and are best served chilled. *Also pictured on page 30.*

Prep time: 25 minutes plus chilling
Baking time: 45 to 47 minutes
● *Degree of difficulty: moderate*

Crumb Crust
- 1 cup all-purpose flour
- 1 cup finely chopped pecans
- ⅓ cup firmly packed brown sugar
- ¼ teaspoon cinnamon
- ¼ teaspoon salt
- ⅓ cup butter *or* margarine, melted
- 1 jar (12 ounces) seedless raspberry jam, stirred until smooth, divided

Cheesecake Filling
- 2 packages (8 ounces each) cream cheese, at room temperature
- ¾ cup granulated sugar
- ½ teaspoon vanilla extract
- ½ teaspoon grated lemon peel
- 3 large eggs

Sour Cream Topping
- 1½ cups sour cream
- 3 tablespoons granulated sugar
- 1 teaspoon vanilla extract

1 Preheat oven to 350°F. Grease a 13x9-inch baking pan.

2 For Crumb Crust, combine the flour, pecans, brown sugar, cinnamon, and salt in a medium bowl. Gradually pour in the butter, tossing with a fork until mixture is moistened. Pat crumb mixture into prepared pan. Bake 15 minutes. Leave oven on.

3 Cool the crust on a wire rack 5 minutes, then carefully spread the top with ¾ cup raspberry jam and cool completely.

4 For Cheesecake Filling, beat the cream cheese, sugar, vanilla, and lemon peel in a large mixing bowl at medium speed until smooth. Add the eggs, one at a time, beating well after each addition. Pour the filling evenly over the jam and spread with a spatula. Bake 25 minutes. Cool 5 minutes. Leave oven on.

5 For Sour Cream Topping, stir sour cream, sugar, and vanilla in a small bowl until smooth. Spread the topping evenly over the warm cheesecake.

6 Warm the remaining jam in a saucepan over medium heat. Carefully pour it into a plastic food storage bag; snip off one end. Pipe the jam in a thin stream on top of the sour cream layer in a swirl pattern. Bake 5 to 7 minutes more, until topping is set. Cool completely in the pan on a wire rack. Refrigerate at least 1 hour or overnight. Cut into 1½x1-inch bars. Makes 6 dozen.

PER COOKIE		DAILY GOAL
Calories	85	2,000 (F), 2,500 (M)
Total Fat	5 g	60 g or less (F), 70 g or less (M)
Saturated fat	2 g	20 g or less (F), 23 g or less (M)
Cholesterol	20 mg	300 mg or less
Sodium	41 mg	2,400 mg or less
Carbohydrates	9 g	250 g or more
Protein	1 g	55 g to 90 g

NOTES

FRESH GINGER-MOLASSES BARS

The grated fresh ginger and translucent brandy glaze are intriguing twists to these cookies.

Prep time: 25 minutes
Baking time: 25 minutes
○ *Degree of difficulty: easy*

2   cups all-purpose flour
½   teaspoon cinnamon
½   teaspoon baking soda
    Pinch salt
½   cup raisins
½   cup vegetable shortening
½   cup butter *or* margarine, softened
¾   cup firmly packed brown sugar
½   cup light molasses
1   large egg
2   tablespoons grated fresh ginger

Brandy Glaze
2   cups sifted confectioners' sugar
3   tablespoons butter *or* margarine, melted
1   tablespoon heavy *or* whipping cream

2   tablespoons brandy *or* cognac
½   teaspoon vanilla extract
    Pinch salt

1   Preheat oven to 375°F. Grease a 13x9-inch baking pan. Combine the flour, cinnamon, baking soda, and salt in a large bowl. Stir in the raisins.

2   Beat the shortening, butter, brown sugar, and molasses in a large mixing bowl at medium speed until light and fluffy. Beat in the egg until smooth. Add the ginger. Beat in the flour mixture at low speed just until blended. Spread batter in prepared pan. Bake 25 minutes, until a toothpick inserted in center comes out clean.

3   For the Brandy Glaze, meanwhile, combine the confectioners' sugar, butter, cream, brandy, vanilla, and salt in a medium bowl until smooth. Pour the glaze evenly over the hot bars. Cool completely in the pan on a wire rack. Cut into 2x1-inch bars. Makes 54.

PER COOKIE		DAILY GOAL
Calories	95	2,000 (F), 2,500 (M)
Total Fat	5 g	60 g or less (F), 70 g or less (M)
Saturated fat	2 g	20 g or less (F), 23 g or less (M)
Cholesterol	11 mg	300 mg or less
Sodium	45 mg	2,400 mg or less
Carbohydrates	13 g	250 g or more
Protein	1 g	55 g to 90 g

CASHEW BARS

Roasted cashews make this a shortbread cookie with a difference.

Prep time: 15 minutes
Baking time: 35 minutes
○ *Degree of difficulty: easy*

¾   cup butter, softened
    (no substitutions)
1   cup firmly packed brown sugar
1   large egg yolk
1   teaspoon vanilla extract
2   cups all-purpose flour
1   cup roasted salted cashews, chopped
30   cashew halves, for garnish

1   Preheat oven to 350°F. Grease a 13x9-inch baking pan. Beat the butter and brown sugar in a large mixing bowl at medium speed until light and fluffy. Beat in the egg yolk and vanilla. Beat in the flour at low speed just until blended. Fold in chopped cashews with a rubber spatula.

2 Spread batter in prepared pan, rolling it flat with a straight-sided glass. Press cashew halves into dough. Bake 35 minutes, until top is golden. Cool completely in the pan on a wire rack. Cut into 2½x1½-inch bars. Makes 30.

ER COOKIE		DAILY GOAL
Calories	130	2,000 (F), 2,500 (M)
Total Fat	7 g	60 g or less (F), 70 g or less (M)
Saturated fat	3 g	20 g or less (F), 23 g or less (M)
Cholesterol	19 mg	300 mg or less
Sodium	79 mg	2,400 mg or less
Carbohydrates	15 g	250 g or more
Protein	2 g	55 g to 90 g

NOTES

THE BEST OF THE BARS

1. Be sure to use the correct size baking pan called for in the recipe. A pan that is too small will cause your bars to be too thick and gummy;, too large a pan will produce thin, dried-out bars.

2. We recommend metal baking pans, because glass absorbs and retains more heat and can cause bars to overbake.

3. Bake bar cookies on the middle rack in the center of the oven.

4. Line the baking pan with foil for the easiest cookie removal and storage. Turn the pan upside down. Tear a strip of foil that will extend 6 inches beyond the length of the pan. Center the foil over the pan, shiny-side up, then gently press the foil down and over the sides and corners of the pan. Lift off the foil and turn the pan over right side up. Gently press the molded foil into the inside of the pan and grease pan as directed. After the bars have cooled completely, use the ends of the foil to lift the cookie from the pan.

5. For most of these recipes, the bar cookies are transferred to a wire rack and cooled completely in the pan. Some shortbread-style bars are cut while still warm in the pan, to prevent excess crumbling.

6. For crisp, multi-layered bars and squares, be sure each layer is cooled completely before adding any topping or filling.

7. To cut bar cookies like a pro, line the baking pan with foil and cool completely in the pan before cutting. Mark the sides of the pan or bar cookie with toothpicks, using a ruler as a guide, then cut the bars with a long sharp or serrated knife.

8. Bar cookies may be stored uncut in the pan and many can be cut and wrapped individually.

9. Testing for doneness of brownies is an art. Insert a toothpick in the center of the pan, a few moist crumbs should still be clinging to it, because the brownies will continue to bake and set as they cool. Be careful not to overbake.

COCONUT-PECAN BARS

Brown sugar in both the shortbread crust and the pecan-coconut topping give these buttery bars a wonderful butterscotch flavor.

Prep time: 25 minutes
Baking time: 40 to 45 minutes
○ *Degree of difficulty: easy*
❄ *Can be frozen up to 3 months*

Shortbread Crust

2 cups all-purpose flour
½ teaspoon salt
¾ cup butter, softened
   (no substitutions)
½ cup firmly packed brown sugar
1 teaspoon vanilla extract
1 large egg yolk

Topping

1¼ cups firmly packed brown sugar
3 large eggs
1 teaspoon vanilla extract
3 tablespoons all-purpose flour
¼ teaspoon salt
1½ cups chopped pecans
¾ cup shredded sweetened coconut

1 Preheat oven to 350°F. For Shortbread Crust, combine the flour and salt in a medium bowl. Beat the butter, brown sugar, and vanilla in a large mixing bowl at medium speed until light and fluffy. Beat in the egg yolk. Beat in flour mixture at low speed just until combined. With lightly floured fingertips, press dough evenly in a 15½x10½-inch jelly-roll pan. Bake 20 minutes, until golden. Cool on a wire rack 5 minutes. Leave oven on.

2 Meanwhile, for Topping, combine brown sugar, eggs, and vanilla in a large mixing bowl. Beat at medium speed until light and fluffy. Beat in the flour and salt at low speed just until combined. Stir in the pecans and coconut. Spread the topping evenly over the baked Shortbread Crust. Bake 20 to 25 minutes more. Cool completely in the pan on a wire rack. Cut into 2½x1-inch bars. Makes 5 dozen.

PER COOKIE		DAILY GOAL
Calories	90	2,000 (F), 2,500 (M)
Total Fat	5 g	60 g or less (F), 70 g or less (M)
Saturated fat	2 g	20 g or less (F), 23 g or less (M)
Cholesterol	20 mg	300 mg or less
Sodium	59 mg	2,400 mg or less
Carbohydrates	11 g	250 g or more
Protein	1 g	55 g to 90 g

NOTES

39

CHOCOLATE-TOFFEE BARS

Three glorious layers, one more delectable than the next, are combined to create this heavenly bar that's almost like candy.

Prep time: 35 minutes plus cooling and chilling
Baking time: 25 to 30 minutes
● *Degree of difficulty: moderate*

Crust
1¾   **cups all-purpose flour**
¼   **cup granulated sugar**
7   **tablespoons butter, cut up (no substitutions)**
1   **large egg**
1   **teaspoon water**
½   **teaspoon vanilla extract**

Toffee Layer
2   **cups chopped walnuts**
1   **cup granulated sugar**
½   **cup heavy *or* whipping cream**
¾   **cup butter, cut into 12 pieces (no substitutions)**
4   **squares (4 ounces) semisweet chocolate, coarsely chopped**

1   Preheat oven to 375°F. For crust, line a 13x9-inch baking pan with foil. Combine the flour, sugar, and butter in a food processor and process until coarse crumbs are formed. Add the egg, water, and vanilla and process, pulsing the machine on and off, until the dough begins to form a ball. Pat dough into prepared pan and bake 25 to 30 minutes, until golden. Cool completely in the pan on a wire rack.

2   For Toffee Layer, reduce oven temperature to 350°F. Spread the walnuts on a baking sheet in a single layer. Bake 8 to 10 minutes, until the nuts are lightly browned and fragrant. Cool. Cook the sugar 8 to 10 minutes, in a large heavy skillet over medium heat, swirling pan occasionally, until completely melted and syrup is a deep caramel color. With a long-handled spoon, quickly and carefully stir in the cream until smooth (mixture may bubble rapidly). Stir in the butter, 3 pieces at a time, until melted. Stir in the toasted walnuts, then pour the mixture immediately over the cooled crust. Spread evenly and let stand until toffee is completely cooled.

3   Melt the chocolate in the top of a double boiler over simmering water, then spread it evenly over the toffee layer. Refrigerate bars one hour until chocolate is set. Cut into 2x1-inch bars. Makes 54.

PER COOKIE		DAILY GOAL
Calories	115	2,000 (F), 2,500 (M)
Total Fat	8 g	60 g or less (F), 70 g or less (M)
Saturated fat	4 g	20 g or less (F), 23 g or less (M)
Cholesterol	18 mg	300 mg or less
Sodium	44 mg	2,400 mg or less
Carbohydrates	10 g	250 g or more
Protein	1 g	55 g to 90 g

NOTES

BLONDIE BARS

Here are our favorite butterscotch brownies, dressed up with chocolate chips and toasted, chopped almonds, all on a buttery shortbread crust.

Prep time: 25 minutes
Baking time: 50 to 55 minutes
Degree of difficulty: easy
Can be frozen up to 3 months

1   cup chopped almonds

Shortbread Crust
2   cups all-purpose flour
½   teaspoon salt
¾   cup butter, softened
       (no substitutions)
¾   cup confectioners' sugar
1   teaspoon vanilla extract

Blondie Topping
1½   cups all-purpose flour
1½   teaspoons baking powder
½   teaspoon salt
¾   cup butter, softened
       (no substitutions)
⅔   cup granulated sugar
⅔   cup firmly packed brown sugar
¼   teaspoon almond extract
3   large eggs
1   cup semisweet chocolate chips

1   Preheat oven to 350°F. Spread the almonds on a baking sheet in a single layer. Bake 8 to 10 minutes, until the nuts are lightly browned and fragrant. Cool. Leave the oven on.

2   For Shortbread Crust, combine the flour and salt in a medium bowl. Beat the butter, confectioners' sugar, and vanilla in a large mixing bowl at medium speed until light and fluffy. Beat in flour mixture at low speed just until combined. With lightly floured fingertips, press dough evenly in a 15½x10½-inch jelly-roll pan. Bake 20 minutes, until golden. Cool on a wire rack 5 minutes.

3   Meanwhile, for Blondie Topping, combine the flour, baking powder, and salt in a medium bowl. Beat the butter, granulated sugar, brown sugar, and almond extract in a large mixing bowl at medium speed until light and fluffy. Beat in the eggs, one at a time, beating well after each addition. Beat in flour mixture just until combined. Stir in the toasted almonds and chocolate chips. Spread the topping over the crust. Bake 30 to 35 minutes, until golden. Cool completely in the pan on a wire rack. Cut into 2x1-inch bars. Makes 6 dozen.

PER COOKIE		DAILY GOAL
Calories	100	2,000 (F), 2,500 (M)
Total Fat	6 g	60 g or less (F), 70 g or less (M)
Saturated fat	3 g	20 g or less (F), 23 g or less (M)
Cholesterol	19 mg	300 mg or less
Sodium	84 mg	2,400 mg or less
Carbohydrates	12 g	250 g or more
Protein	1 g	55 g to 90 g

NOTES

CINNAMON SLEDGES

With treats this easy to prepare, it's no wonder these cinnamon-packed, crisp cookie bars are one of our most requested recipes ever.

Prep time: 20 minutes
Baking time: 40 to 45 minutes
O *Degree of difficulty: easy*
❄ *Can be frozen up to 2 months*

2 **cups all-purpose flour**
1 **tablespoon cinnamon**
⅛ **teaspoon salt**
1 **cup butter *or* margarine, softened**
½ **cup firmly packed brown sugar**
½ **cup granulated sugar**
1 **large egg, separated**
1½ **cups chopped pecans**

1 Preheat oven to 300°F. Combine the flour, cinnamon, and salt in a bowl. Beat the butter, brown sugar, granulated sugar, and egg yolk in a large mixing bowl at medium speed until light and fluffy. Beat in the flour mixture at low speed just until blended (mixture will be stiff).

2 With lightly floured fingertips, press dough into an ungreased 15½x10½-inch jelly-roll pan. Beat the egg white with a fork in a small bowl just until foamy. Brush evenly on top of dough. Sprinkle the dough with the pecans and press in lightly. Bake 40 to 45 minutes, until top is golden. Transfer the pan to a wire rack. While still hot, cut the cookie into 3-inch squares, then cut diagonally into triangles. Cool completely in the pan on a wire rack. Makes 30.

PER COOKIE		DAILY GOAL
Calories	150	2,000 (F), 2,500 (M)
Total Fat	10 g	60 g or less (F), 70 g or less (M)
Saturated fat	4 g	20 g or less (F), 23 g or less (M)
Cholesterol	24 mg	300 mg or less
Sodium	75 mg	2,400 mg or less
Carbohydrates	14 g	250 g or more
Protein	2 g	55 g to 90 g

NOTES

CLASSIC LEMON SQUARES

Our secret for these best-ever lemon bars is a touch of baking powder in the curd topping, which gives you the pure taste of lemon and a cakey texture.

Prep time: 15 minutes
Baking time: 40 minutes
O *Degree of difficulty: easy*

Crust
½ cup butter *or* margarine, softened
¼ cup granulated sugar
1¼ cups all-purpose flour

Topping
2 large eggs, lightly beaten
¾ cup granulated sugar
3 tablespoons fresh lemon juice
2 tablespoons all-purpose flour
1 teaspoon grated lemon peel
¼ teaspoon baking powder
   Confectioners' sugar

1 Preheat oven to 350°F. For Crust, beat the butter and the sugar in a medium bowl with a wooden spoon until creamy. Gradually stir in the flour. Press dough evenly in the bottom of an ungreased 9-inch square baking pan. Bake 20 to 25 minutes, until golden.

2 Meanwhile, for Topping, whisk together eggs, the sugar, lemon juice, flour, lemon peel, and baking powder in a medium bowl. Pour the lemon mixture over the hot crust. Return to oven and bake 12 to 15 minutes more, until set. Cool completely in the pan on a wire rack. Just before serving, sift confectioners' sugar on top. Cut into 16 squares. Makes 16.

PER COOKIE		DAILY GOAL
Calories	150	2,000 (F), 2,500 (M)
Total Fat	6 g	60 g or less (F), 70 g or less (M)
Saturated fat	4 g	20 g or less (F), 23 g or less (M)
Cholesterol	42 mg	300 mg or less
Sodium	74 mg	2,400 mg or less
Carbohydrates	22 g	250 g or more
Protein	2 g	55 g to 90 g

LEMON-WALNUT COOKIE BRITTLE

These cookies are wonderful served with a fresh fruit sorbet. During humid weather, store them in the freezer and sprinkle them with confectioners' sugar just before serving.

Prep time: 20 minutes
Baking time: 25 to 28 minutes
O *Degree of difficulty: easy*
❄ *Can be frozen up to 1 month*

1 **cup butter, softened (no substitutions)**
1 **cup plus 1 tablespoon confectioners' sugar**
1 **teaspoon grated lemon peel**
¼ **teaspoon salt**
2 **cups all-purpose flour**
½ **cup finely chopped walnuts**

1 Preheat oven to 325°F. Beat the butter in a large mixing bowl at medium speed until smooth. Beat in 1 cup of the confectioners' sugar until fluffy. Beat in the lemon peel and salt. Beat in the flour at low speed until well combined. Stir in the walnuts (mixture will be crumbly).

2 With lightly floured fingertips, press dough into an ungreased 15½x10½-inch jelly-roll pan, leaving the edges slightly thicker. Bake 25 to 28 minutes, until top is completely golden. Cool completely in the pan on a wire rack. Sift the remaining 1 tablespoon confectioners' sugar on top. Break into chunks as desired. Makes 50 2x1½-inch cookies.

PER COOKIE		DAILY GOAL
Calories	70	2,000 (F), 2,500 (M)
Total Fat	4 g	60 g or less (F), 70 g or less (M)
Saturated fat	2 g	20 g or less (F), 23 g or less (M)
Cholesterol	10 mg	300 mg or less
Sodium	48 mg	2,400 mg or less
Carbohydrates	7 g	250 g or more
Protein	1 g	55 g to 90 g

CHOCOLATE-PECAN DIAMONDS

Chock full of pecans with just a touch of fudginess, these elegant diamond-shaped cookies are perfect alongside a bowl of fresh fruit or ice cream.

Ⓜ *Microwave*
    Prep time: 15 minutes
    Baking time: 40 minutes
○ *Degree of difficulty: easy*
❋ *Can be frozen up to 1 month*

¾ **cup butter, softened
      (no substitutions)**
½ **cup confectioners' sugar**
½ **teaspoon salt**
2 **cups all-purpose flour**

Filling
2 **squares (2 ounces) unsweetened
      chocolate, chopped**
4 **large eggs**
1½ **cups firmly packed brown sugar**
3 **cups (12 ounces) pecans, chopped**
2 **teaspoons vanilla extract**
½ **teaspoon salt**

1 Preheat oven to 375°F. Beat the butter, confectioners' sugar, and salt in a large mixing bowl at medium speed until light and fluffy. Beat in the flour at low speed just until blended.

2 With lightly floured fingertips, press dough into the bottom of an ungreased 15½x10½-inch jelly-roll pan. Bake 20 minutes, until top is golden. Cool on a wire rack 5 minutes. Reduce oven temperature to 350°F.

3 Meanwhile, for Filling, place the chocolate in a small microwave-proof bowl. Microwave on medium (50% power) 1½ to 2 minutes, stirring every minute, until chocolate begins to melt. Remove the bowl from the microwave and continue to stir until the chocolate is completely melted. Beat the eggs and brown sugar in a large mixing bowl at medium speed just until blended. Stir in the melted chocolate, pecans, vanilla, and salt.

4 Pour the filling over the hot crust. Bake 20 minutes. Cool completely in the pan on a wire rack. Cut crosswise into 1½-inch strips, then cut strips diagonally at 2-inch intervals to form diamonds. Makes 4 dozen.

PER COOKIE		DAILY GOAL
Calories	135	2,000 (F), 2,500 (M)
Total Fat	9 g	60 g or less (F), 70 g or less (M
Saturated fat	3 g	20 g or less (F), 23 g or less (M
Cholesterol	25 mg	300 mg or less
Sodium	83 mg	2,400 mg or less
Carbohydrates	14 g	250 g or more
Protein	2 g	55 g to 90 g

NOTES

SANTA FE BROWNIES

The Plaza Bakery in Santa Fe created these cream cheese-filled brownies and they became an instant favorite of dessert queen Maida Heatter. Extra-tall and luscious, we fell in love with them too. For easiest cutting, refrigerate these beauties overnight.

Prep time: 40 minutes plus chilling
Baking time: 1 hour 20 minutes
Degree of difficulty: moderate
Can be frozen up to 1 month

1	cup plus 1 teaspoon butter
6	squares (6 ounces) unsweetened chocolate, coarsely chopped
6	squares (6 ounces) semisweet chocolate, coarsely chopped
1½	cups all-purpose flour
1½	teaspoons baking powder
¾	teaspoon salt
5	large eggs
1½	cups firmly packed brown sugar
1¼	cups granulated sugar
1	tablespoon vanilla extract
1½	cups walnuts, broken into large pieces

Cream Cheese Mixture

12	ounces cream cheese, at room temperature
6	tablespoons butter, softened (no substitutions)
1½	teaspoons vanilla extract
¾	cup granulated sugar
3	large eggs

1 Preheat oven to 350°F. Line a 13x9-inch baking pan with foil. Melt 1 teaspoon of the butter and brush the bottom and sides of the pan with it. Melt the unsweetened chocolate, semisweet chocolate, and the remaining 1 cup butter in top of a double boiler over simmering water. Set mixture aside and cool slightly.

2 Stir together the flour, baking powder, and salt in a medium bowl. Beat the eggs in a large mixing bowl at medium speed until just blended. Add the brown sugar, granulated sugar, and vanilla; beat just until smooth. Beat in the chocolate mixture, then flour mixture, at low speed just until combined. Reserve 2¼ cups batter. Stir the walnuts into remaining batter in the mixing bowl. Spread the batter in the prepared pan.

3 For Cream Cheese Mixture, beat the cream cheese and butter in a clean mixing bowl at medium speed until smooth. Gradually beat in the vanilla and sugar until light and fluffy. Add the eggs, one at a time, beating well after each addition and beat just until smooth. Spoon the mixture over the chocolate batter in prepared pan, spreading to edges of the pan.

4 Stir reserved chocolate batter to soften. Spoon the batter over the cream cheese layer. With a knife, cut through batters in a zigzag pattern to marbleize slightly. Bake 1 hour 20 minutes, until toothpick inserted in center comes out barely clean. (If the top browns too quickly during baking, cover the pan loosely with foil.) Cool completely in the pan on a wire rack. Invert onto a cookie sheet; gently lift off pan and remove foil. Invert again, cover tightly with plastic wrap and refrigerate overnight.

5 With a long, sharp knife, cut brownies into quarters, then cut each quarter into 8 squares. Makes 32.

PER COOKIE		DAILY GOAL
Calories	330	2,000 (F), 2,500 (M)
Total Fat	21 g	60 g or less (F), 70 g or less (M)
Saturated fat	11 g	20 g or less (F), 23 g or less (M)
Cholesterol	87 mg	300 mg or less
Sodium	207 mg	2,400 mg or less
Carbohydrates	33 g	250 g or more
Protein	5 g	55 g to 90 g

ONE-BOWL BROWNIES

In the years since Katherine Hepburn shared her easy saucepan brownie recipe with us, it has remained a favorite of both our staff and readers. We've made it quicker by melting the chocolate in the microwave.

Ⓜ   *Microwave*
    Prep time: 10 minutes
    Baking time: 40 minutes
Ⓞ   *Degree of difficulty: easy*
✳   *Can be frozen up to 3 months*

- 1 **cup chopped walnuts *or* pecans**
- 3 **squares (3 ounces) unsweetened chocolate, chopped**
- ½ **cup butter *or* margarine, cut up**
- 1 **cup granulated sugar**
- 2 **large eggs**
- ½ **teaspoon vanilla extract**
- ½ **cup all-purpose flour**
- ¼ **teaspoon salt**

1 Preheat oven to 350°F. Arrange the walnuts in an 8-inch square baking pan and bake 10 minutes, until toasted and fragrant. Cool them completely in the pan then remove walnuts and set aside.

2 Reduce oven temperature to 325°F. Grease and flour the baking pan; tap to remove the excess flour.

3 Combine the chocolate and butter in a large microwave-proof bowl. Microwave on high (100% power) 1½ minutes or until melted. Stir in the sugar, then the eggs and vanilla and beat until well combined. Stir in the flour and salt. Fold in the toasted walnuts. Bake 40 minutes, until center is just set. Cool completely in the pan on a wire rack. Cut into 2-inch squares. Makes 16.

PER COOKIE		DAILY GOAL
Calories	200	2,000 (F), 2,500 (M)
Total Fat	14 g	60 g or less (F), 70 g or less (M)
Saturated fat	6 g	20 g or less (F), 23 g or less (M)
Cholesterol	43 mg	300 mg or less
Sodium	103 mg	2,400 mg or less
Carbohydrates	18 g	250 g or more
Protein	3 g	55 g to 90 g

DRIZZLE BROWNIES

The simple drizzled topping of melted white chocolate sets these rich, dark finger treats apart. If you want to freeze these brownies, add the topping the day you plan to serve them.

Ⓜ   *Microwave*
    Prep time: 20 minutes
    Baking time: 30 minutes
Ⓞ   *Degree of difficulty: easy*
❄   *Can be frozen up to 3 months*

1½   **cups chopped walnuts**
 8   **squares (8 ounces) unsweetened
      chocolate, coarsely chopped**
¾   **cup butter *or* margarine, cut up**
1½   **teaspoons vanilla extract**
 3   **cups granulated sugar**
 6   **large eggs**
¼   **teaspoon salt**
1½   **cups all-purpose flour**
 3   **ounces white chocolate, coarsely
      chopped**

1 Preheat oven to 350°F. Spread the walnuts on a baking sheet in a single layer. Bake 8 to 10 minutes, until lightly browned and fragrant. Cool.

2 Line a 15½x10½-inch jelly-roll pan with foil and grease the foil. Combine the unsweetened chocolate and butter in a medium saucepan. Melt over medium heat, stirring occasionally. Stir in the vanilla; remove from heat and cool.

3 Increase oven temperature to 375°F. Beat the sugar, eggs, and salt in a large mixing bowl at medium speed until light and fluffy. Add the chocolate mixture and beat until blended. Beat in flour at low speed until smooth. Stir in the toasted walnuts. Spoon batter into prepared pan.

4 Bake 35 minutes, until a toothpick inserted in the center comes out clean. Cool in the pan on a wire rack 30 minutes. Invert the brownies onto another rack. Carefully lift off the pan and remove the foil. Invert the brownies again on a rack and cool completely right side up.

5 Place the white chocolate in a small plastic food storage bag and microwave on low (30% power) 6 to 8 minutes, kneading every 2 minutes, until it is melted and

smooth. Snip one corner from the bag and pipe the chocolate decoratively over the top of the brownies. Let them stand until white chocolate is set. Cut into 1½-inch squares. Makes 70.

PER COOKIE		DAILY GOAL
Calories	105	2,000 (F), 2,500 (M)
Total Fat	6 g	60 g or less (F), 70 g or less (M)
Saturated fat	3 g	20 g or less (F), 23 g or less (M)
Cholesterol	24 mg	300 mg or less
Sodium	36 mg	2,400 mg or less
Carbohydrates	13 g	250 g or more
Protein	2 g	55 g to 90 g

NOTES

OLD-TIME MINNESOTA BARS

As easy as a cup of cocoa, these homey brownies from cookbook author Phillip Stephen Schulz became an instant hit in our test kitchen. If your kids aren't crazy about nuts, simply omit them.

Prep time: 15 minutes
Baking time: 25 minutes
○ *Degree of difficulty: easy*
❄ *Can be frozen up to 2 months*

½   **cup all-purpose flour**
½   **cup unsweetened cocoa powder**
¼   **teaspoon baking powder**
¼   **teaspoon salt**
½   **cup butter** *or* **margarine, softened**
1   **cup granulated sugar**
1   **teaspoon vanilla extract**
2   **large eggs**
½   **cup chopped pecans** *or* **walnuts**

1 Preheat oven to 350°F. Grease an 8-inch square baking pan. Combine the flour, cocoa, baking powder, and salt in a small bowl. Set aside.

2 Beat the butter in a large mixing bowl at medium speed until creamy. Gradually beat in the sugar, then the vanilla until the batter is light and fluffy. Add the eggs, one at a time, beating well after each addition. Beat in flour mixture at low speed just until blended. Stir in the pecans.

3 Spoon the batter into prepared pan. Bake 25 minutes, until a toothpick inserted in the center comes out barely clean. Cool completely in the pan on a wire rack. Cut into 2-inch squares. Makes 16.

PER COOKIE		DAILY GOAL
Calories	155	2,000 (F), 2,500 (M)
Total Fat	9 g	60 g or less (F), 70 g or less (M)
Saturated fat	4 g	20 g or less (F), 23 g or less (M)
Cholesterol	42 mg	300 mg or less
Sodium	107 mg	2,400 mg or less
Carbohydrates	18 g	250 g or more
Protein	2 g	55 g to 90 g

NOTES

51

ONLY

CHOCOLATE

Cookie eaters love chocolate! They love cookies mixed with cocoa, dipped in a bittersweet glaze, freckled with chips, or studded with chunks. This chapter is chock full of chocolate choices, from Chipperdoodles to White-Chocolate Cherry-Chunk Cookies. Sink your teeth into these fudgy temptations. We guarantee you'll come back for more!

PECAN-CHOCOLATE CHIP BARS

This chewy treat resembles a classic chocolate chip cookie baked in bar form.

Prep time: 15 minutes plus cooling
Baking time: 25 minutes
○ *Degree of difficulty: easy*
❋ *Can be frozen up to 3 months*

1¾ cups all-purpose flour
½ teaspoon salt
1 cup butter, softened
    (no substitutions)
1½ cups firmly packed brown sugar
1 teaspoon vanilla extract
2 large eggs
1 package (12 ounces) semisweet
    chocolate chips, divided
1½ cups coarsely chopped pecans,
    divided

1 Preheat oven to 375°F. Combine the flour and salt in a small bowl. Beat the butter and brown sugar in a large mixing bowl at medium speed until light and fluffy. Beat in the vanilla. Add the eggs, one at a time, beating well after each addition.

With mixer at low speed, gradually add flour mixture. Stir in 1½ cups of the chocolate chips and ¾ cup of the chopped pecans.

2 Spoon batter into an ungreased 15½x10½-inch jelly-roll pan. Sprinkle with the remaining ½ cups chocolate chips and ¾ cup chopped pecans. Bake 25 minutes, until a toothpick inserted in the center comes out clean. Cool completely in the pan on a wire rack. Cut into 2½x1½-inch bars. Makes 42.

PER COOKIE		DAILY GOAL
Calories	155	2,000 (F), 2,500 (M)
Total Fat	10 g	60 g or less (F), 70 g or less (M)
Saturated fat	4 g	20 g or less (F), 23 g or less (M)
Cholesterol	22 mg	300 mg or less
Sodium	77 mg	2,400 mg or less
Carbohydrates	18 g	250 g or more
Protein	1 g	55 g to 90 g

CHOCOLATE CHIP COOKIE BARK

Chocolate chip lovers may want to use both semisweet and white chocolate chips in these goodies—but remember, white chocolate burns more easily than dark. That's why you must add the white chips toward the end of baking.

Prep time: 15 minutes
Baking time: 25 minutes
○ *Degree of difficulty: easy*
❋ *Can be frozen up to 1 month*

2 cups all-purpose flour
½ teaspoon salt
¾ cup butter *or* margarine, softened
¼ cup vegetable shortening
1 cup granulated sugar
1 teaspoon vanilla extract
1 package (12 ounces) semisweet
    chocolate chips *or* 1½ cups
    semisweet chocolate chips and
    ½ cup white chocolate chips,
    divided
½ cup old-fashioned oats, uncooked,
    divided
½ cup chopped walnuts, optional

1 Preheat oven to 375°F. Grease a 15½x10½-inch jelly-roll pan.

2 Combine the flour and salt in a medium bowl. Beat the butter, shortening, sugar, and vanilla in a large mixing bowl at medium speed until light and fluffy, scraping the bowl occasionally with a rubber spatula. Gradually beat in flour mixture at low speed until well combined. Stir in 1 cup of the semisweet chocolate hips and ¼ cup of the oats. Pat dough into prepared pan. Sprinkle the remaining ¼ cup oats, the walnuts, and the remaining 1 cup of chocolate chips (or ½ cup if using white chocolate chips, too) over the top; press lightly into dough.

3 Bake 25 minutes, until edges are lightly browned. (Note: If using white chocolate chips, bake 25 minutes; add white chips and bake 2 minutes more.) Cool completely in the pan on a wire rack. Break into 2x1-inch pieces. Makes 6 dozen.

PER COOKIE		DAILY GOAL
Calories	75	2,000 (F), 2,500 (M)
Total Fat	4 g	60 g or less (F), 70 g or less (M)
Saturated fat	2 g	20 g or less (F), 23 g or less (M)
Cholesterol	5 mg	300 mg or less
Sodium	35 mg	2,400 mg or less
Carbohydrates	9 g	250 g or more
Protein	1 g	55 g to 90 g

NOTES

CHAMPION CHOCOLATE CHIP COOKIES

Nothing beats the real thing! These blue-ribbon winners will have the whole family raiding the cookie jar time and time again.

Prep time: 20 minutes
Baking time: 12 minutes per batch
○ *Degree of difficulty: easy*
❄ *Can be frozen up to 3 months*

1 **cup chopped pecans**
2¼ **cups all-purpose flour**
1 **teaspoon baking soda**
1 **teaspoon salt**
½ **cup butter, softened (no substitutions)**
½ **cup vegetable shortening**
1 **cup granulated sugar**
½ **cup firmly packed brown sugar**
2 **large eggs**
1 **teaspoon vanilla extract**
1 **package (12 ounces) semisweet chocolate chips**

1 Preheat oven to 375°F. Spread the pecans on a baking sheet in a single layer. Bake 6 to 8 minutes, until lightly browned and fragrant. Cool. Leave oven on.

2 Combine the flour, baking soda, and salt in a medium bowl. Beat the butter, shortening, granulated sugar, and brown sugar in a large mixing bowl at medium speed until light and fluffy. Beat in the eggs, one at a time, beating well after each addition. Beat in the vanilla. Beat in flour mixture at low speed just until combined. Stir in the chocolate chips and toasted pecans.

3 Drop batter by heaping teaspoonfuls onto 2 ungreased cookie sheets. Bake 12 minutes, until golden. Transfer the cookies to wire racks to cool completely. Makes 6 dozen.

PER COOKIE		DAILY GOAL
Calories	90	2,000 (F), 2,500 (M)
Total Fat	5 g	60 g or less (F), 70 g or less (M)
Saturated fat	2 g	20 g or less (F), 23 g or less (M)
Cholesterol	9 mg	300 mg or less
Sodium	64 mg	2,400 mg or less
Carbohydrates	11 g	250 g or more
Protein	1 g	55 g to 90 g

WHITE-CHOCOLATE CHUNK-CHERRY COOKIES

These cocoa drops are studded with chunks of white chocolate, dried cherries, and chopped pecans. They're a special treat when prepared with imported white chocolate bars, but you can also use 1 cup of white chocolate chips. *Also pictured on page 52.*

Prep time: 20 minutes
Baking time: 8 to 10 minutes per batch
Degree of difficulty: easy
Can be frozen up to 3 months

- 1 **cup all-purpose flour**
- ¼ **cup unsweetened cocoa powder**
- 1 **teaspoon baking powder**
- ¼ **teaspoon salt**
- ½ **cup butter** *or* **margarine, softened**
- 1 **cup granulated sugar**
- 1 **large egg**
- ½ **teaspoon vanilla extract**
- 6 **ounces white chocolate, coarsely chopped**
- 1 **cup chopped pecans**
- ½ **cup dried cherries** *or* **raisins**

1 Preheat oven to 350°F. Grease 2 cookie sheets. Combine the flour, cocoa, baking powder, and salt in a medium bowl. Beat the butter in a large mixing bowl at medium speed until smooth. Gradually beat in sugar until light and fluffy. Beat in the egg and vanilla until blended. Beat in flour mixture at low speed just until combined. Stir in the white chocolate, pecans, and dried cherries.

2 Drop dough by teaspoonfuls 2 inches apart onto prepared cookie sheets. Bake 8 to 10 minutes, until tops are just firm. Transfer the cookies to wire racks to cool completely. Makes 5 dozen.

PER COOKIE		DAILY GOAL
Calories	65	2,000 (F), 2,500 (M)
Total Fat	4 g	60 g or less (F), 70 g or less (M)
Saturated fat	2 g	20 g or less (F), 23 g or less (M)
Cholesterol	8 mg	300 mg or less
Sodium	38 mg	2,400 mg or less
Carbohydrates	8 g	250 g or more
Protein	1 g	55 g to 90 g

DOUBLE CHOCOLATE COOKIES

A plate of these extra-large cookies, studded with semisweet chocolate and served warm, are sure to satisfy the child in all of us. This handy dough keeps in the refrigerator up to a week, so you can make it ahead and bake off a batch in no time.

Prep time: 10 minutes
Baking time: 12 to 14 minutes
per batch

O *Degree of difficulty: easy*

½	**cup walnuts *or* pecans**
¾	**cup all-purpose flour**
⅓	**cup unsweetened cocoa powder**
¼	**teaspoon baking soda**
¼	**teaspoon salt**
6	**tablespoons butter *or* margarine, softened**
⅓	**cup granulated sugar**
⅓	**firmly packed brown sugar**
2	**tablespoons milk**
1	**teaspoon vanilla extract**
½	**cup semisweet chocolate chips**

1 Preheat oven to 350°F. Spread the walnuts on a baking sheet in a single layer. Bake 8 to 10 minutes, until lightly browned and fragrant. Cool the walnuts and coarsely chop them. Leave oven on.

2 Combine the flour, cocoa, baking soda, and salt in a medium bowl. Beat the butter, granulated sugar, and brown sugar in a large mixing bowl at medium speed until light and fluffy. Beat in the milk and vanilla until blended. Beat in flour mixture at low speed just until combined. Stir in the chocolate chips and walnuts. (Can be made ahead. Wrap and refrigerate batter up to 1 week.)

3 Grease 2 cookie sheets. Spoon batter by heaping tablespoonfuls onto prepared cookie sheets. Bake 12 to 14 minutes, until set in centers. Cool on cookie sheets 2 minutes, then transfer cookies to wire racks to cool slightly. Serve warm. Makes 15 cookies.

PER COOKIE		DAILY GOAL
Calories	160	2,000 (F), 2,500 (M)
Total Fat	10 g	60 g or less (F), 70 g or less (M)
Saturated fat	4 g	20 g or less (F), 23 g or less (M)
Cholesterol	13 mg	300 mg or less
Sodium	107 mg	2,400 mg or less
Carbohydrates	20 g	250 g or more
Protein	2 g	55 g to 90 g

HOW TO MELT CHOCOLATE

Melting chocolate is easy, but it requires some care and gentle heating. Chocolate that is overheated may scorch or turn coarse and grainy. White and milk chocolates, which have a higher quantity of milk solids, need to be stirred sooner and more frequently than unsweetened or semisweet varieties.

Double Boiler Method: Place chopped chocolate in the top of a double boiler, then place the pan top in the pan bottom over hot, but not simmering water. The bottom of the top pan should not be touching the water. Melt the chocolate, stirring occasionally, until smooth. Remove the top of the double boiler from the bottom, making sure the chocolate never comes in contact with any steam or water.

Microwave Method: Place chopped chocolate in a microwave-proof bowl. Microwave on medium (50% power) 1½ to 3 minutes, stirring every minute, until chocolate begins to melt. Remove from the microwave and stir until chocolate is completely melted.

THE BEST CHOCOLATE CHUNK COOKIES

It's chocolate heaven! These double-the-nuts, fudgy bites take the chocolate chip cookie to a whole new level of indulgence. Just like your favorite brownie, be sure not to overbake these. They will become firm as they cool.

Prep time: 30 minutes plus cooling
Baking time: 7 to 8 minutes per batch
Degree of difficulty: easy
Can be frozen up to 1 month

1½ **cups chopped walnuts**
1½ **cups chopped pecans**
8 **squares (8 ounces) semisweet chocolate, coarsely chopped**
3 **squares (3 ounces) unsweetened chocolate, coarsely chopped**
½ **cup unsalted butter, cut up (no substitutions)**
⅔ **cup all-purpose flour**
½ **teaspoon baking powder**
¼ **teaspoon salt**

3 **large eggs, at room temperature**
1¼ **cups granulated sugar**
2 **teaspoons vanilla extract**
1½ **cups semisweet chocolate chips**

Glaze
4 **squares (4 ounces) semisweet chocolate, coarsely chopped**

1 Preheat oven to 325°F. Spread the walnuts and pecans on a baking sheet in a single layer. Bake 8 to 10 minutes, until lightly browned and fragrant. Cool. Leave oven on.

2 Melt the semisweet and unsweetened chocolates with the butter in a double boiler over hot, not boiling, water until smooth. Remove from heat and set aside to cool.

3 Grease 2 cookie sheets. Combine the flour, baking powder, and salt in a medium bowl. Beat the eggs and sugar in a large mixing bowl at medium-high speed for 10 minutes, until a ribbon forms when the beaters are lifted. Beat in the melted chocolate mixture and vanilla at medium speed. Stir in flour mixture just until combined (do not overmix). Stir in the chocolate chips and nuts.

4 Drop batter by teaspoonfuls 2 inches apart onto prepared cookie sheets. Bake 7 to 8 minutes, until barely firm and tops are slightly cracked. Cool the cookies on cookie sheets 2 minutes then transfer them to wire racks to cool completely.

5 For Glaze, melt semisweet chocolate in a double boiler over hot, not boiling, water until smooth. Remove from heat and cool slightly. Dip 1 side of the cooled cookies in the melted chocolate. Return the cookies to wire racks and let stand until chocolate is set. Makes 4 dozen.

PER COOKIE		DAILY GOAL	
Calories	170	2,000 (F), 2,500 (M)	
Total Fat	12 g	60 g or less (F), 70 g or less (M)	
Saturated fat	4 g	20 g or less (F), 23 g or less (M)	
Cholesterol	19 mg	300 mg or less	
Sodium	21 mg	2,400 mg or less	
Carbohydrates	16 g	250 g or more	
Protein	2 g	55 g to 90 g	

NOTES

59

PEANUT BUTTER-CHOCOLATE CHIP COOKIES

Chocolate and peanut butter are favorites with big and little kids alike. Use any variety of peanut butter you please.

Prep time: 10 minutes
Baking time: 11 to 13 minutes
*   per batch*
O   *Degree of difficulty: easy*
❅   *Can be frozen up to 3 months*

2¼ **cups all-purpose flour**
  1 **teaspoon baking soda**
  ½ **teaspoon salt**
  ⅔ **cup peanut butter**
  ½ **cup vegetable shortening**
1½ **cups granulated sugar**
  2 **large eggs**
  2 **tablespoons milk**
  1 **teaspoon vanilla extract**
  1 **package (6 ounces) semisweet
        chocolate chips**

1 Preheat oven to 375°F. Grease 2 cookie sheets. Combine the flour, baking soda, and salt in a medium bowl. Beat the peanut butter, shortening, and sugar in a large mixing bowl at medium speed until light and fluffy. Add the eggs, one at a time, beating well after each addition. Beat in the milk and vanilla. Beat in flour mixture at low speed just until combined. Stir in the chocolate chips.

2 Drop dough by heaping teaspoonfuls onto prepared cookie sheets. Bake 11 to 13 minutes, until golden. Transfer the cookies to wire racks to cool completely. Makes 4½ dozen.

PER COOKIE		DAILY GOAL
Calories	95	2,000 (F), 2,500 (M)
Total Fat	5 g	60 g or less (F), 70 g or less (M)
Saturated fat	1 g	20 g or less (F), 23 g or less (M)
Cholesterol	8 mg	300 mg or less
Sodium	53 mg	2,400 mg or less
Carbohydrates	12 g	250 g or more
Protein	2 g	55 g to 90 g

NOTES

TRIPLE CHOCOLATE CHIPPERS

Chunks of white chocolate join semisweet chocolate chips in these moist cocoa drops.

Prep time: 20 minutes
Baking time: 12 to 15 minutes per
*   batch*
○ *Degree of difficulty: easy*
❊ *Can be frozen up to 2 months*

¾ **cup all-purpose flour**
¼ **cup unsweetened cocoa powder**
1 **teaspoon baking powder**
¼ **teaspoon salt**
½ **cup butter *or* margarine, softened**
1 **cup granulated sugar**
1 **large egg**
½ **teaspoon vanilla extract**
1 **package (6 ounces) semisweet**
    chocolate chips
3 **ounces white chocolate, chopped**
½ **cup chopped almonds**

1 Preheat oven to 350°F. Grease 2 cookie sheets. Combine the flour, cocoa, baking powder, and salt in a medium bowl. Beat the butter and sugar in a large mixing bowl at medium speed until light and fluffy. Beat in the egg and vanilla. Beat in flour mixture at low speed just until blended. Stir in the chocolate chips, white chocolate, and nuts.

2 Drop dough by teaspoonfuls 2 inches apart onto prepared cookie sheets. Bake 12 to 15 minutes, until firm. Cool cookies on cookie sheets 5 minutes; transfer to wire racks to cool. Makes 3 dozen.

PER COOKIE		DAILY GOAL
Calories	100	2,000 (F), 2,500 (M)
Total Fat	6 g	60 g or less (F), 70 g or less (M)
Saturated fat	3 g	20 g or less (F), 23 g or less (M)
Cholesterol	13 mg	300 mg or less
Sodium	61 mg	2,400 mg or less
Carbohydrates	13 g	250 g or more
Protein	1 g	55 g to 90 g

CHOCOLATE CANDY DROPS

Prep time: 20 minutes
Baking time: 12 to 15 minutes per
*   batch*
○ *Degree of difficulty: easy*

¾ **cup all-purpose flour**
¼ **cup unsweetened cocoa powder**
1 **teaspoon baking powder**
¼ **teaspoon salt**
½ **cup butter *or* margarine, softened**
1 **cup granulated sugar**
1 **large egg**
½ **teaspoon vanilla extract**
2 **cups candy-coated chocolate**
    candies

1 Preheat oven to 350°F. Grease 2 cookie sheets. Combine the flour, cocoa, baking powder, and salt in a bowl. Beat the butter and sugar in a large mixing bowl at medium speed until light and fluffy. Beat in egg and vanilla until blended. Beat in flour mixture at low speed just until combined. Stir in candies.

2 Drop batter by teaspoonfuls 2 inches apart onto prepared cookie sheets. Bake 12 to 15 minutes, until firm. Transfer to wire racks to cool. Makes 4 dozen.

PER COOKIE		DAILY GOAL
Calories	90	2,000 (F), 2,500 (M)
Total Fat	4 g	60 g or less (F), 70 g or less (M)
Saturated fat	1 g	20 g or less (F), 23 g or less (M)
Cholesterol	11 mg	300 mg or less
Sodium	52 mg	2,400 mg or less
Carbohydrates	12 g	250 g or more
Protein	1 g	55 g to 90 g

CHIPPERDOODLES

You'll love their crackly cinnamon-sugar coating on these homey chocolate chip cookies.

Prep time: 15 minutes
Baking time: 10 minutes per batch
O *Degree of difficulty: easy*
❄ *Can be frozen up to 1 month*

2¾ **cups all-purpose flour**
2 **teaspoons cream of tartar**
1 **teaspoon baking soda**
¼ **teaspoon salt**
1 **cup butter, softened**
   (no substitutions)
1¼ **cups plus 2 tablespoons granulated**
   sugar, divided
2 **large eggs**
1 **package (12 ounces) semisweet**
   chocolate chips
2 **teaspoons cinnamon**

1 Preheat oven to 400°F. Combine the flour, cream of tartar, baking soda, and salt in a medium bowl. Beat the butter and 1¼ cups of the sugar in a large mixing bowl at medium speed until light and fluffy. Beat in the eggs, one at a time, beating well after each addition. Beat in flour mixture at low speed just until combined. Stir in the chocolate chips.

2 Combine the remaining 2 tablespoons sugar with the cinnamon in a small bowl. Shape dough into 1½-inch balls and roll in cinnamon-sugar mixture.

3 Drop dough by teaspoonfuls 2 inches apart onto ungreased cookie sheets. Flatten the balls slightly with the bottom of a glass. Bake 10 minutes, until firm. Immediately transfer the cookies to wire racks to cool completely. Makes 3 dozen.

PER COOKIE		DAILY GOAL
Calories	160	2,000 (F), 2,500 (M)
Total Fat	8 g	60 g or less (F), 70 g or less (M)
Saturated fat	5 g	20 g or less (F), 23 g or less (M)
Cholesterol	26 mg	300 mg or less
Sodium	106 mg	2,400 mg or less
Carbohydrates	21 g	250 g or more
Protein	2 g	55 g to 90 g

PERFECT DROP COOKIES

1. For quick and easy cookies, the most important thing to remember is to keep the size of the cookies uniform for even baking. Using the right kind of spoon makes all the difference, and in most of our recipes we call for a flatware teaspoon or tablespoon with a level amount of dough.

2. "Rounded" is about 1½ times the level measure of dough. "Heaping" is about twice the amount of dough that would fit on a level teaspoon or tablespoon.

3. Drop cookies are made of a soft dough and many recipes can be easily prepared with a large wooden spoon instead of a mixer. Just be sure your butter or shortening is sufficiently softened, and it's helpful if the other ingredients are at room temperature.

THE ULTIMATE CHOCOLATE CHUNK COOKIES

These are cookies for the sophisticated sweet tooth.... crisp and buttery, with chunks of bittersweet chocolate and toasted hazelnuts, cookies simply can't get better than these. *Also pictured on the cover.*

Prep time: 20 minutes
Baking time: 12 to 14 minutes
    per batch
O   Degree of difficulty: easy
❋   Can be frozen up to 3 months

1   **cup whole hazelnuts**
2   **cups all-purpose flour**
1   **teaspoon baking soda**
½   **teaspoon salt**
1¼ **cups firmly packed brown sugar**
1   **cup unsalted butter, softened**
       (no substitutions)
2   **large eggs**
1   **teaspoon vanilla extract**
8   **ounces bittersweet chocolate** *or*
       8 squares (8 ounces) semisweet
       chocolate, cut into ½-inch
       chunks

1 Preheat oven to 350°F. Spread the hazelnuts on a baking sheet in a single layer. Bake 12 to 15 minutes, until lightly browned and skins are crackly. Wrap nuts in a clean kitchen towel and let them stand 5 minutes. Rub the nuts in the towel to remove their skins, then cool completely and chop coarsely. Leave oven on.

2 Combine the flour, baking soda, and salt in a medium bowl. Beat the brown sugar and butter in a large mixing bowl at medium speed until light and fluffy. Add the eggs, one at a time, beating well after each addition, then beat in the vanilla. Beat in flour mixture at low speed just until combined. Stir in the chocolate and nuts.

3 Drop dough by heaping teaspoonfuls onto ungreased cookie sheets. Bake 12 to 14 minutes, until lightly browned. Transfer the cookies to wire racks to cool completely. Makes 3 dozen.

PER COOKIE		DAILY GOAL
Calories	155	2,000 (F), 2,500 (M)
Total Fat	9 g	60 g or less (F), 70 g or less (M)
Saturated fat	4 g	20 g or less (F), 23 g or less (M)
Cholesterol	26 mg	300 mg or less
Sodium	73 mg	2,400 mg or less
Carbohydrates	17 g	250 g or more
Protein	2 g	55 g to 90 g

NOTES

65

CHOCOLATE MINTS

If green chocolate mints aren't available, you can use a minty milk chocolate bar with chocolate cookie bits or any other kind of solid chocolate mint bar.

Prep time: 40 minutes plus chilling
Baking time: 12 to 13 minutes
*   per batch*
O *Degree of difficulty: easy*
❄ *Can be frozen up to 1 month*

¾ **cup butter *or* margarine**
1½ **cups firmly packed dark**
      brown sugar
2 **tablespoons water**
1 **package (12 ounces) semisweet**
      chocolate chips
2½ **cups all-purpose flour**
1¼ **teaspoons baking soda**
½ **teaspoon salt**
2 **large eggs**
      Green chocolate mint wafers
      (about 1 pound)

1 Heat the butter, brown sugar, and water in a large, heavy saucepan over low heat until butter is melted. Add the chocolate chips and cook, stirring, until partially melted. Remove from heat and continue stirring until the chocolate is completely melted. Pour the chocolate mixture into a large mixing bowl and let stand about 10 minutes to cool slightly.

2 Combine the flour, baking soda, and salt in a medium bowl. Beat the eggs, one at a time, into the chocolate mixture at medium speed. Beat in the flour mixture at low speed just until combined. Refrigerate until dough is firm, about 1 hour.

3 Preheat oven to 350°F. Line 2 cookie sheets with foil. Roll teaspoonfuls of dough into balls; place about 2 inches apart on cookie sheets. Bake 12 to 13 minutes, until the tops are firm. Remove from oven and immediately place a mint wafer on each hot cookie. Let the mint soften, then with a small spatula, swirl mint over cookies to frost. Decorate with shaved mint wafers. Transfer the cookies to wire racks to cool completely. Makes 80.

PER COOKIE		DAILY GOAL
Calories	100	2,000 (F), 2,500 (M)
Total Fat	5 g	60 g or less (F), 70 g or less (M)
Saturated fat	4 g	20 g or less (F), 23 g or less (M)
Cholesterol	10 mg	300 mg or less
Sodium	58 mg	2,400 mg or less
Carbohydrates	13 g	250 g or more
Protein	1 g	55 g to 90 g

NOTES

CHOCOLATE-PEANUT BUTTER SANDWICHES

Melted peanut butter chips make an instant creamy filling in these extra-rich double chocolate drops.

Ⓜ Microwave
  Prep time: 40 minutes plus chilling
  Baking time: 8 to 10 minutes
     per batch
○ *Degree of difficulty: easy*

1   **cup all-purpose flour**
¼   **cup unsweetened cocoa powder**
1   **teaspoon baking powder**
¼   **teaspoon salt**
½   **cup butter *or* margarine, softened**
1   **cup granulated sugar**
1   **large egg**
½   **teaspoon vanilla extract**
1   **package (12 ounces) peanut**
       butter chips
4   **squares (4 ounces) semisweet**
       chocolate, coarsely chopped

1 Combine the flour, cocoa, baking powder, and salt in a medium bowl. Beat the butter in a large mixing bowl at medium speed until smooth. Gradually beat in the sugar until light and fluffy. Beat in the egg and vanilla until blended. Beat in flour mixture at low speed just until combined. Refrigerate dough 15 minutes.

2 Preheat oven to 350°F. Grease 2 cookie sheets. Roll dough into 1-inch balls. Place 2 inches apart on prepared cookie sheets. Lightly press the top of each ball to flatten. Bake 8 to 10 minutes. Transfer the cookies to wire racks to cool completely.

3 Place the peanut butter chips in a medium microwave-proof bowl. Microwave on medium (50% power) 1½ to 3 minutes, stirring every minute, until chips begin to melt. Remove the bowl from the microwave and continue to stir until chips are completely melted. Spread the melted chips on the bottoms of half the cooled cookies, then top with the remaining cookies to make sandwiches.

4 Place semisweet chocolate in another medium microwave-proof bowl. Microwave on medium (50% power) 1½ to 3 minutes, stirring every minute, until chocolate begins to melt. Remove the bowl from the microwave and continue to stir until chocolate is completely melted. Dip each cookie sandwich halfway into the melted chocolate and transfer them to wire racks. Let stand until chocolate is set. Makes 2½ dozen.

PER COOKIE		DAILY GOAL	
Calories	150	2,000 (F), 2,500 (M)	
Total Fat	8 g	60 g or less (F), 70 g or less (M)	
Saturated fat	3 g	20 g or less (F), 23 g or less (M)	
Cholesterol	15 mg	300 mg or less	
Sodium	95 mg	2,400 mg or less	
Carbohydrates	18 g	250 g or more	
Protein	3 g	55 g to 90 g	

NOTES

CHOCOLATE CRINKLES

These pretty confections are a super chocolate sensation with a touch of coffee flavor. They're even better the next day—if they last that long.

Prep time: 20 minutes plus chilling
Baking time: 10 to 12 minutes
      per batch
O   *Degree of difficulty: easy*
❋   *Can be frozen up to 3 months*

½   **cup butter *or* margarine, cut up**
4   **squares (4 ounces) unsweetened chocolate, coarsely chopped**
1   **teaspoon instant coffee powder (optional)**
2   **cups all-purpose flour**
2   **teaspoons baking powder**
½   **teaspoon salt**
2   **cups granulated sugar**
4   **large eggs**
1½ **teaspoons vanilla extract**
1   **cup confectioners' sugar**

1 Melt the butter and chocolate with the coffee, if desired, in a double boiler over hot, not boiling, water until smooth. Remove from heat and set aside to cool slightly.

2 Combine the flour, baking powder, and salt in a medium bowl. Beat the chocolate mixture and granulated sugar in a large mixing bowl at medium speed just until combined. Add the eggs, one at a time, beating well after each addition, then beat in vanilla. Beat in flour mixture at low speed just until combined. Refrigerate at least 2 hours, until dough is very firm.

3 Preheat oven to 350°F. Grease 2 cookie sheets. Place the confectioners' sugar on a plate. Drop chilled dough by teaspoonfuls onto sugar and roll into balls. Place balls 2 inches apart on prepared cookie sheets. Bake 10 to 12 minutes, until the tops are just set *(do not overbake)*. Cool the cookies on cookie sheets 1 minute, then transfer them to wire racks to cool completely. Makes 5 dozen.

PER COOKIE		DAILY GOAL
Calories	80	2,000 (F), 2,500 (M)
Total Fat	3 g	60 g or less (F), 70 g or less (M)
Saturated fat	2 g	20 g or less (F), 23 g or less (M)
Cholesterol	18 mg	300 mg or less
Sodium	56 mg	2,400 mg or less
Carbohydrates	12 g	250 g or more
Protein	1 g	55 g to 90 g

LIKE COCOA FOR CHOCOLATE

To substitute cocoa for unsweetened chocolate, use 3 tablespoons unsweetened cocoa plus 1 tablespoon butter, vegetable shortening, or vegetable oil for each 1-ounce square of chocolate.

NOTES

HAZELNUT-CHOCOLATE CRESCENTS

In a favorite recipe given to us by cookbook author Michele Urvater, chocolate shortbread dough is filled with hazelnuts and molded into dainty crescents. Store these cookies in an airtight container, preferably in the refrigerator.

Prep time: 30 minutes plus chilling
Baking time: 15 to 20 minutes
*   per batch*
O   *Degree of difficulty: easy*

1   **cup hazelnuts**
5   **squares (5 ounces) semisweet chocolate, coarsely chopped, divided**
8   **tablespoons granulated sugar, divided**
2   **cups all-purpose flour**
¼   **teaspoon salt**
¾   **cup plus 2 tablespoons butter, softened (no substitutions), divided**

1 Preheat oven to 350°F. Spread the hazelnuts on a baking sheet in a single layer. Bake 12 to 15 minutes, until lightly browned and skins are crackly. Wrap nuts in a clean kitchen towel and let stand 5 minutes. Rub the nuts in the towel to remove skins, then cool completely.

2 Melt 3 squares of the chocolate in a double boiler over hot, not boiling, water until smooth. Remove from heat and set aside to cool.

3 Process the nuts and 2 tablespoons of the sugar in a food processor until fine. Transfer to a medium bowl and combine with the flour and salt. Beat the butter and the remaining 6 tablespoons sugar in a large mixing bowl at medium speed until light and fluffy. Beat in the melted chocolate until blended, then add the nut mixture and combine. Cover and refrigerate until firm, 2 hours.

4 Preheat oven to 350°F. Grease 2 cookie sheets. Shape teaspoonfuls of dough into crescents. Arrange 2 inches apart on prepared cookie sheets. Bake 15 to 20 minutes. Transfer the cookies to wire racks to cool completely.

5 To decorate, melt the remaining 2 squares chocolate in a double boiler over hot, not boiling, water until smooth. Remove from heat. Drizzle over the tops o the cookies; let stand until chocolate is set. Makes 4 dozen.

PER COOKIE		DAILY GOAL
Calories	85	2,000 (F), 2,500 (M)
Total Fat	6 g	60 g or less (F), 70 g or less (M
Saturated fat	3 g	20 g or less (F), 23 g or less (M
Cholesterol	9 mg	300 mg or less
Sodium	48 mg	2,400 mg or less
Carbohydrates	8 g	250 g or more
Protein	1 g	55 g to 90 g

NOTES

CHOCOLATE-CINNAMON MERINGUES

Chocolate flavored meringues? Yes indeed! With a touch of cinnamon and a dip in melted chocolate, these elegant cookies are a breeze to make with a pastry bag.

Prep time: 30 minutes plus cooling
Baking time: 1 hour 15 minutes
Degree of difficulty: moderate

2 **large egg whites, at room temperature**
¼ **teaspoon cream of tartar**
⅛ **teaspoon salt**
½ **cup granulated sugar**
½ **teaspoon vanilla extract**
3 **tablespoons unsweetened cocoa powder**
¼ **teaspoon cinnamon**
4 **squares (4 ounces) semisweet chocolate, coarsely chopped**

1 Preheat oven to 225°F. Line 2 cookie sheets with foil.

2 Beat the egg whites in a large mixing bowl at medium speed until foamy. Add the cream of tartar and salt and continue to beat until soft peaks form. Gradually beat in the sugar, one tablespoon at a time, then continue to beat until stiff. Beat in the vanilla. Gently fold the cocoa and cinnamon into whites with a rubber spatula just until blended.

3 Spoon the meringue into a large pastry bag fitted with a #47 large basket-weave tip. Pipe into 3-inch lengths onto prepared cookie sheets. Bake 1 hour 15 minutes. Turn oven off. Cool in oven at least 1½ hours or overnight.

4 Melt the chocolate in the top of a double boiler over simmering water. Carefully peel the meringues from the foil. Dip one tip of each meringue into melted chocolate. Transfer the cookies to wire racks and let stand until chocolate is set. Makes 3½ dozen.

PER COOKIE		DAILY GOAL
Calories	20	2,000 (F), 2,500 (M)
Total Fat	1 g	60 g or less (F), 70 g or less (M)
Saturated fat	.5 g	20 g or less (F), 23 g or less (M)
Cholesterol	0 mg	300 mg or less
Sodium	10 mg	2,400 mg or less
Carbohydrates	4 g	250 g or more
Protein	0 g	55 g to 90 g

NOTES

HERITAGE

TRADITIONS

Many of our most intriguing cookies are legacies from other countries, passed from mother to daughter through the generations. We've raided those ancestral cookie jars to bring you this sensational collection of sweet treats. Inspired by baking traditions across the globe, this cookie sampler salutes treasured old-world recipes. Here are the glorious cookies that immigrated to the United States.

RYE COOKIE CUT-OUTS

Ultra-thin and crisp, these Finnish delicacies are a tasty way to use rye flour, and you'll love their slightly nutty flavor.

Prep time: 10 minutes
Baking time: 5 to 7 minutes per batch
◑ *Degree of difficulty: moderate*
❄ *Can be frozen up to 3 months*

1 **cup all-purpose flour**
⅓ **cup rye flour**
⅛ **teaspoon salt**
½ **cup unsalted butter, softened (no substitutions)**
⅓ **cup granulated sugar**

1 Combine the all-purpose and rye flours and salt in a medium bowl. Beat the butter and sugar in a large mixing bowl at medium speed until light and fluffy. Gradually beat in flour mixture at low speed just until blended.

2 Preheat oven to 375°F. Grease 2 cookie sheets. On a lightly floured surface with a floured rolling pin, roll dough ⅛ inch thick. Cut with a floured 2-inch plain or scalloped cookie cutter. Transfer to prepared cookie sheets and prick each cookie with a fork. Bake 5 to 7 minutes, until lightly browned. Transfer the cookies to wire racks to cool completely. Makes 2½ dozen.

PER COOKIE		DAILY GOAL
Calories	55	2,000 (F), 2,500 (M)
Total Fat	3 g	60 g or less (F), 70 g or less (M)
Saturated fat	2 g	20 g or less (F), 23 g or less (M)
Cholesterol	9 mg	300 mg or less
Sodium	12 mg	2,400 mg or less
Carbohydrates	6 g	250 g or more
Protein	1 g	55 g to 90 g

NOTES

ROSETTES

The key to making these very delicate fried cookies from Sweden is heating the oil to the correct temperature. Rosette irons can be purchased at good kitchenware stores.

Prep time: 5 minutes plus chilling
Baking time: 30 minutes
● *Degree of difficulty: moderate*

- 1 **cup all-purpose flour**
- 2 **tablespoons granulated sugar**
  Pinch salt
- 2 **large eggs**
- 1 **cup milk**
- 2 **quarts vegetable oil**
- ¾ **cup sifted confectioners' sugar**

1 Combine the flour, granulated sugar, and salt in a medium bowl. In another bowl, lightly beat the eggs and milk until blended. Gradually whisk the milk mixture into dry ingredients until smooth. Cover and refrigerate 1 hour.

2 Heat the oil in a Dutch oven or large saucepan over medium-high heat to 375°F. Dip the rosette iron into hot oil. Tap off excess oil and dip iron into batter until iron is about three-fourths covered (do not immerse completely). Fry the batter until rosette slips off iron. Remove iron and continue to fry cookie until golden, about 40 seconds total. (If the rosette does not come off the iron, carefully remove it with a fork.) With a slotted spoon, transfer rosette to paper towels to drain. Repeat frying cookies, heating the iron each time and stirring the batter before dipping.

3 When rosettes are cool, sprinkle with confectioners' sugar. Store in an airtight container at room temperature up to 1 week. Makes 6 dozen.

PER COOKIE		DAILY GOAL
Calories	35	2,000 (F), 2,500 (M)
Total Fat	3 g	60 g or less (F), 70 g or less (M)
Saturated fat	0 g	20 g or less (F), 23 g or less (M)
Cholesterol	6 mg	300 mg or less
Sodium	5 mg	2,400 mg or less
Carbohydrates	3 g	250 g or more
Protein	0 g	55 g to 90 g

KRUMKAKE

Although there are many European versions of a very flat, wafer-thin butter cookie with an embossed design, we're especially fond of this one from Norway. *Also pictured on page 72.*

Prep time: 15 minutes plus standing
Cooking time: 45 to 90 seconds
per cookie
⬤ *Degree of difficulty: moderate*

1½ **cups all-purpose flour**
¼ **teaspoon cardamom**
⅛ **teaspoon salt**
1 **cup granulated sugar**
6 **tablespoons unsalted butter, softened (no substitutions)**
2 **large eggs, at room temperature**
⅔ **cup milk**
⅓ **cup heavy *or* whipping cream**
1 **teaspoon vegetable shortening**

1 Combine the flour, cardamom, and salt in a medium bowl. Beat the sugar and butter in a large mixing bowl at medium speed until blended. Add the eggs, one at a time, beating well after each addition. Add dry ingredients, then the milk and cream, beating until smooth. Let stand 30 minutes.

2 Meanwhile, heat a stovetop krumkake iron over medium heat or preheat an electric krumkake iron according to manufacturers' directions. Lightly brush the inside of the iron with shortening. Spoon 1 tablespoon of the batter in the center; close iron and cook 45 seconds. If using stovetop iron, turn iron over and cook 35 to 45 seconds more, until lightly browned. Transfer the cookie to a wire rack. While still warm, carefully roll cookie into a cone or cigar shape. Cool completely. Repeat process with remaining batter. Store in airtight container up to one week. Makes 3 dozen.

PER COOKIE		DAILY GOAL
Calories	75	2,000 (F), 2,500 (M)
Total Fat	3 g	60 g or less (F), 70 g or less (M)
Saturated fat	2 g	20 g or less (F), 23 g or less (M)
Cholesterol	21 mg	300 mg or less
Sodium	15 mg	2,400 mg or less
Carbohydrates	10 g	250 g or more
Protein	1 g	55 g to 90 g

SPECULAAS

We used an old-fashioned cookie mold to give these wonderful almond-spice cookies from Belgium a classic design. For the holidays, decorate these cookies with Confectioners' Icing (see recipe, page 114).

Prep time: 20 minutes plus chilling
Baking time: 16 to 18 minutes
● *Degree of difficulty: moderate*
❄ *Can be frozen up to 3 months*

3½ **cups all-purpose flour**
½ **cup ground blanched almonds**
2 **teaspoons cinnamon**
1 **teaspoon ginger**
½ **teaspoon nutmeg**
¼ **teaspoon baking soda**
¼ **teaspoon salt**
¼ **teaspoon cloves**
1 **cup unsalted butter, softened**
    (no substitutions)
1½ **cups granulated sugar**
2 **large eggs**
½ **teaspoon grated lemon peel**

1 Combine the flour, almonds, cinnamon, ginger, nutmeg, baking soda, salt, and cloves in a large bowl. Beat the butter and sugar in a large mixing bowl at medium speed until light. Add the eggs, one at a time, beating until light and fluffy. Beat in the lemon peel. Gradually beat in flour mixture at low speed until blended. Pat dough into a disk; wrap and refrigerate 4 hours or overnight.

2 Preheat oven to 350°F. Grease 2 cookie sheets. Divide the dough into quarters. Lightly coat speculaas mold* with vegetable cooking spray. Sprinkle with flour, tapping out excess. Between 2 sheets of lightly floured wax paper, roll one quarter of dough ⅓ inch thick (keep remaining dough refrigerated). Remove the top sheet of wax paper.

3 Invert dough over the prepared mold. Gently press the dough into mold with rolling pin to remove any air; lift off remaining wax paper. Trim edge of dough, then tap mold gently against work surface to loosen. Carefully unmold dough. With a wide metal spatula, transfer the cookie to a prepared cookie sheet. Repeat the process with remaining dough, rerolling scraps.

Arrange the cookies 2 inches apart on prepared cookie sheets.

4 Bake 16 to 18 minutes, until edges are golden and tops are firm when pressed lightly with fingertip. Transfer the cookies to wire racks to cool completely. Makes 2 dozen 2-inch cookies.

PER COOKIE		DAILY GOAL
Calories	205	2,000 (F), 2,500 (M)
Total Fat	10 g	60 g or less (F), 70 g or less (M)
Saturated fat	5 g	20 g or less (F), 23 g or less (M)
Cholesterol	39 mg	300 mg or less
Sodium	41 mg	2,400 mg or less
Carbohydrates	27 g	250 g or more
Protein	3 g	55 g to 90 g

NOTES

CLASSIC SHORTBREAD

These very British shortbread cookies are quite tender, so you can shape them any way you like.

Prep time: 25 minutes
Baking time: 20 to 25 minutes
 per batch
○ *Degree of difficulty: easy*
❄ *Can be frozen up to 3 months*

2½ **cups all-purpose flour**
 Pinch salt
 1 **cup unsalted butter**
  (no substitutions)
 1 **cup confectioners' sugar**

1 Preheat oven to 325°F. Combine the flour and salt in a medium bowl. Beat the butter and confectioners' sugar in a large mixing bowl at medium speed until light and fluffy. Gradually beat in flour mixture at low speed just until combined.

2 Knead the dough lightly on work surface. Divide dough in half. Place half of the dough in the center of an ungreased cookie sheet. Sprinkle the dough lightly with flour and cover with a sheet of wax paper. Roll into an 8¼-inch circle, ¼ inch thick. Remove the wax paper. Press an inverted 8-inch round cake pan or tart pan into dough to form an 8-inch circle with a straight or scalloped edge. (If using a cake pan, trim the edge with a small knife.) Cut another circle in the center of dough with a 2-inch round cookie cutter, leaving it in place. Divide the outer ring into 8 equal wedges with a pastry wheel or knife. Prick each wedge and center circle with a fork. Repeat process with the remaining dough.

3 Bake 20 to 25 minutes, until edges are lightly golden. While shortbread is still hot, recut it into wedges. Transfer it to a wire rack to cool completely. Makes 18.

PER COOKIE		DAILY GOAL
Calories	180	2,000 (F), 2,500 (M)
Total Fat	10 g	60 g or less (F), 70 g or less (M)
Saturated fat	6 g	20 g or less (F), 23 g or less (M)
Cholesterol	60 mg	300 mg or less
Sodium	9 mg	2,400 mg or less
Carbohydrates	20 g	250 g or more
Protein	2 g	55 g to 90 g

PACKING COOKIES

1. Cookies that hit the road need to be sturdy. Bar cookies, drop cookies, slice and bake cookies, and some hand-molded cookies are the best candidates for traveling.

2. If you are sending an assortment of cookies, always wrap spice, soft, and crisp cookies separately to preserve their textures and so the flavors don't mingle.

3. Pack cookies in rigid containers such as tins, decorated coffee or shortening cans, heavy-duty plastic containers, or cardboard boxes. Pack the cookies close together in a single layer between sheets of wax paper, padding packing with crumbled wax paper or paper towels on the top to prevent shifting. For assorted cookies, place the heavier cookies on the bottom.

4. Be creative decorating your cookie container. Choose from purchased decorative cookie tins, colored bags, gift boxes and assorted ribbons.

BASLER BRUNSLI

s befits their alpine origin, these crisp chocolate-nut confections, flavored with a int of cinnamon and cloves, are the innacle of Swiss cookies.

Prep time: 40 minutes
Baking time: 12 to 14 minutes
*   per batch*
Degree of difficulty: moderate
Can be frozen up to 3 months

1   **cup hazelnuts**
3   **squares (3 ounces) unsweetened chocolate, coarsely chopped**
1   **cup natural almonds**
4   **cups confectioners' sugar, divided**
½   **teaspoon cinnamon**
⅛   **teaspoon cloves**
⅛   **teaspoon salt**
2   **large egg whites**
1   **square (1 ounces) semisweet chocolate, melted, for decoration**
1   **ounce white chocolate, melted, for decoration**

1   Preheat oven to 350°F. Spread the hazelnuts on a baking sheet in a single layer. Bake 12 to 15 minutes, until lightly browned and skins are crackly. Wrap nuts in a clean kitchen towel and let stand 5 minutes. Rub the nuts in the towel to remove skins, then cool completely.

2   Reduce oven temperature to 325°F. Place the unsweetened chocolate in a food processor and pulse until finely ground. Transfer the chocolate to a sheet of wax paper. Place the hazelnuts and almonds in the processor and pulse until finely ground. Return chocolate to processor with 2½ cups of the confectioners' sugar, cinnamon, cloves, and salt; process until combined. With the machine on, add the egg whites and process until dough just forms a ball.

3   Line 2 cookie sheets with foil. Generously sprinkle work surface with confectioners' sugar. Knead the dough until it is no longer sticky, adding as much of the remaining confectioners' sugar as necessary. Roll dough into a 14x9-inch rectangle, ¼ inch thick, adding more sugar to prevent sticking. Cut into 2½x1-inch diamonds. Transfer the cookies to prepared cookie sheets.

4   Bake 12 to 14 minutes, until slightly firm and puffed *(do not overbake)*. Cool completely on cookie sheets on wire racks. Remove cookies from foil and trim edges if desired. Drizzle with melted chocolates. Makes 4 dozen.

PER COOKIE		DAILY GOAL
Calories	80	2,000 (F), 2,500 (M)
Total Fat	4 g	60 g or less (F), 70 g or less (M)
Saturated fat	1 g	20 g or less (F), 23 g or less (M)
Cholesterol	0 mg	300 mg or less
Sodium	9 mg	2,400 mg or less
Carbohydrates	12 g	250 g or more
Protein	1 g	55 g to 90 g

NOTES

HAZELNUT BISCOTTI

Viva Italia! Biscotti (which means "baked twice") are crisp cookies that are dipped in espresso or sweet wine to eat as a dessert or snack.

Prep time: 30 minutes plus cooling
Baking time: 50 minutes
○ *Degree of difficulty: easy*
❄ *Can be frozen up to 3 months*

- 1 **cup whole hazelnuts *or* natural almonds**
- 3 **cups all-purpose flour**
- 2 **teaspoons baking powder**
- ½ **teaspoon salt**
- ¾ **cup butter *or* margarine, softened**
- 1 **cup granulated sugar**
- 3 **large eggs, at room temperature**
- 1½ **teaspoon grated lemon peel**
- ½ **teaspoon almond extract**

1 Preheat oven to 350°F. Spread the hazelnuts on a baking sheet in a single layer. Bake 12 to 15 minutes, until lightly browned and skins are crackly. Wrap nuts in a clean kitchen towel and let stand 5 minutes. Rub the nuts in the towel to remove skins, then cool completely. (If using almonds, bake 10 minutes; leave skins on.) Chop coarsely. Leave oven on.

2 Grease 1 cookie sheet. Combine the flour, baking powder, and salt in a medium bowl. Beat the butter and sugar in a large mixing bowl at medium speed until light and fluffy. Add the eggs, one at a time, beating well after each addition. Beat in the lemon peel and almond extract. Beat in flour mixture at low speed just until combined. Stir in the nuts.

3 Shape dough into two 12-inch logs and place 4 inches apart on prepared cookie sheet. Bake 25 to 30 minutes, until a toothpick inserted in the center comes out clean. Transfer the logs to wire racks and cool 15 minutes.

4 With a serrated knife, slice the logs diagonally ½ inch thick. Place cut sides down on an ungreased cookie sheet. Bake 12 minutes, until bottoms of cookies turn golden. Turn cookies over and bake 10 to 12 minutes more, until both sides are just golden. Transfer the cookies to wire racks to cool completely. Makes 3½ dozen.

PER COOKIE		DAILY GOAL
Calories	105	2,000 (F), 2,500 (M)
Total Fat	6 g	60 g or less (F), 70 g or less (M)
Saturated fat	2 g	20 g or less (F), 23 g or less (M)
Cholesterol	24 mg	300 mg or less
Sodium	89 mg	2,400 mg or less
Carbohydrates	12 g	250 g or more
Protein	2 g	55 g to 90 g

NOTES

CUCCIDATI

If you love soft, fig-filled cookies, you'll adore these Italian fig cookies. They're best if sliced just before serving.

Prep time: 1½ hours plus chilling and cooling
Baking time: 22 to 28 minutes
Degree of difficulty: moderate
Can be frozen up to 1 month

6 **Granny Smith apples, peeled and finely chopped (8 cups)**
1 **bag (8 ounces) Calimyrna figs, finely chopped (1¾ cups)**
8 **ounces whole pitted dates, finely chopped (1¾ cups)**
½ **cup fresh orange juice**
1⅓ **cups granulated sugar, divided**
1 **cup chopped walnuts**
5 **cups all-purpose flour**
2 **teaspoons baking powder**
1 **teaspoon baking soda**
½ **teaspoon salt**
1 **cup butter *or* margarine, softened**
2 **large eggs**
1 **cup sour cream**
2 **teaspoons vanilla extract**
  Confectioners' sugar

1 Combine the apples, figs, dates, orange juice, and ⅓ cup of the sugar in a large Dutch oven. Cover and cook, stirring occasionally, over medium-low heat 25 minutes, until tender. Cook 5 minutes more, uncovered, stirring until liquid has evaporated. Cool completely. Refrigerate the fruit mixture until ready to assemble cookies. Stir in the walnuts.

2 Grease 2 cookie sheets. Combine the flour, baking powder, baking soda, and salt in a medium bowl. Beat the butter and the remaining 1 cup granulated sugar in a large mixing bowl at medium speed until light. Add the eggs, one at a time, beating until light and fluffy. Beat in the sour cream and vanilla. Gradually beat in flour mixture at low speed until blended. Wrap and refrigerate the dough 1 hour.

3 Preheat oven to 350°F. Divide dough into 8 equal pieces. On a lightly floured surface, roll 1 piece of dough into an 8-inch rope. With a floured rolling pin, roll rope into a 10x5-inch rectangle. Spoon ¾ cup of the filling down the center of the rectangle. Fold the sides over the filling and pinch together to seal. Place the log, seam side down, on a prepared cookie sheet. Repeat process with remaining dough and filling, arranging 4 logs on each cookie sheet.

4 Place cookie sheets on 2 oven racks. Bake logs 22 to 28 minutes, until just golden, switching the pans halfway through. Transfer the logs to wire racks to cool completely. Just before serving, sift confectioners' sugar over logs. Using a serrated knife, cut into ½-inch slices. Makes 12 dozen.

PER COOKIE		DAILY GOAL
Calories	55	2,000 (F), 2,500 (M)
Total Fat	2 g	60 g or less (F), 70 g or less (M)
Saturated fat	1 g	20 g or less (F), 23 g or less (M)
Cholesterol	7 mg	300 mg or less
Sodium	35 mg	2,400 mg or less
Carbohydrates	9 g	250 g or more
Protein	1 g	55 g to 90 g

NOTES

HUNGARIAN POPPY SEED-NUT SLICES

This easy slice-and-bake cookie is packed with crunchy poppy seeds and almonds. It's a great cookie to dunk in coffee or tea.

Prep time: 30 minutes plus chilling
Baking time: 20 minutes per batch
○ *Degree of difficulty: easy*
❄ *Can be frozen up to 3 months*

    2 **cups all-purpose flour**
   ¼ **teaspoon salt**
    1 **cup butter, softened**
          (no substitutions)
    1 **cup plus 2 tablespoons granulated**
          sugar, divided
    1 **large egg**
    1 **teaspoon vanilla extract**
   ½ **teaspoon cinnamon**
  1½ **cups finely chopped almonds**
   ½ **cup poppy seeds**

1 Combine the flour and salt in a medium bowl. Beat the butter and 1 cup of the sugar in a large mixing bowl at medium speed until light. Add the egg, vanilla, and cinnamon and beat 2 to 3 minutes, until light and fluffy. Add the almonds and poppy seeds and beat 1 minute more. Beat in flour mixture at low speed until blended. Cover and refrigerate dough until firm, about 2 hours.

2 Shape the dough into 2 logs about 2 inches in diameter. Roll logs in the remaining 2 tablespoons sugar. Wrap in wax paper and refrigerate 3 hours or overnight.

3 Preheat oven to 325°F. Cut each log into ¼-inch-thick slices. Place slices on ungreased cookie sheets. Bake 20 minutes, until edges begin to brown. Transfer the cookies to wire racks to and cool completely. Makes 6 dozen.

PER COOKIE		DAILY GOAL
Calories	70	2,000 (F), 2,500 (M)
Total Fat	4 g	60 g or less (F), 70 g or less (M)
Saturated fat	2 g	20 g or less (F), 23 g or less (M)
Cholesterol	10 mg	300 mg or less
Sodium	35 mg	2,400 mg or less
Carbohydrates	7 g	250 g or more
Protein	1 g	55 g to 90 g

NOTES

GREEK KOURABIEDES

These S-shaped butter cookies get their
fabulous flavor from the whole clove
inserted in each one.

Prep time: 1 hour plus chilling
Baking time: 15 to 17 minutes
*   per batch*
○ *Degree of difficulty: easy*
❄ *Can be frozen up to 3 months*

¾ **cup blanched slivered almonds**
2 **cups all-purpose flour**
½ **teaspoon baking powder**
¼ **teaspoon salt**
1 **cup unsalted butter, softened**
    (no substitutions)
½ **cup confectioners' sugar**
1 **large egg yolk**
2 **tablespoons brandy**
1 **teaspoon vanilla extract**
¼ **cup whole cloves**
    Additional confectioners' sugar,
    for decoration

1 Preheat oven to 350°F. Spread almonds
on a baking sheet in a single layer. Bake
about 8 minutes, until lightly browned and
fragrant. Cool nuts completely. Place nuts
in a food processor or blender and process
until finely ground.

2 Combine the ground almonds, flour,
baking powder, and salt in a medium bowl.
Beat the butter and confectioners' sugar in
a large mixing bowl at medium speed until
light. Beat in the egg yolk until light and
fluffy. Beat in the brandy and vanilla.
Gradually beat in flour mixture at low
speed just until combined. Wrap and
refrigerate dough 6 hours or overnight.

3 Preheat oven to 325°F. Grease 2 cookie
sheets. On a lightly floured surface, roll the
dough by teaspoonfuls into 4-inch-long
ropes. Arrange 1 rope on a prepared cookie
sheet in an S shape. Repeat with remaining
ropes, placing them 1 inch apart. Gently
press one whole clove in the center of each
cookie. Bake 15 to 17 minutes, until lightly
golden. Transfer the cookies to wire racks
to cool slightly, 5 minutes. Generously sift
additional confectioners' sugar over the
cookies and cool completely. Store in an
airtight container up to one week. Makes
6 dozen.

PER COOKIE		DAILY GOAL
Calories	50	2,000 (F), 2,500 (M)
Total Fat	3 g	60 g or less (F), 70 g or less (M)
Saturated fat	2 g	20 g or less (F), 23 g or less (M)
Cholesterol	10 mg	300 mg or less
Sodium	13 mg	2,400 mg or less
Carbohydrates	4 g	250 g or more
Protein	1 g	55 g to 90 g

NOTES

DUTCH LETTERS

What makes these flaky cookies from the Netherlands so special? The almond-paste centers of course, and the fun you'll have shaping the dough into any letters you want.

Prep time: 1 hour 20 minutes
plus chilling
Baking time: 20 minutes per batch
● *Degree of difficulty: moderate*
❄ *Can be frozen up to 3 months*

3 **cups all-purpose flour**
¼ **teaspoon salt**
1 **cup cold unsalted butter, cut up**
   (no substitutions)
1 **large egg yolk**
6 **to 7 tablespoons ice water**
1 **tube (7 ounces)** *or* **1 can (8 ounces)**
   almond paste
⅓ **cup plus 2 tablespoons granulated**
   sugar, divided
1 **large egg**
¼ **teaspoon grated lemon peel**
1 **large egg white, lightly beaten**

1 Combine the flour and salt in a large bowl. With a pastry blender or 2 knives, cut in the butter until mixture resembles fine crumbs. Blend the egg yolk and 2 tablespoons of ice water in a cup with a fork. Drizzle the egg mixture into flour mixture, tossing with the fork. Add remaining ice water, one tablespoon at a time, tossing just until pastry holds together. Divide pastry into quarters. Press each quarter into a 4-inch square. Wrap and refrigerate 1 hour or overnight.

2 Beat the almond paste, ⅓ cup of the sugar, egg, and lemon peel in a large mixing bowl until light and fluffy. Spoon the filling into a heavy-duty plastic storage bag and seal. Refrigerate until slightly firm, 1 hour or overnight.

3 Preheat oven to 375°F. Between 2 sheets of lightly floured wax paper, roll one quarter of the pastry into a 9½-inch square about ⅛ inch thick. With a ruler and a sharp knife, trim the pastry to a 9-inch square, then cut it into four 2¼x9-inch strips. Lightly brush 1 strip with water. Snip one corner of the plastic bag with scissors and pipe the filling in a ½-inch-thick stripe down the center of the pastry strip, leaving a ½-inch border of pastry at both ends. Fold one long side of pastry over filling; fold the opposite side over and gently press edges to seal. Place pastry roll, seam side down on a ungreased cookie sheet. Shape into an S or other letter.

4 Brush the top of the letter with lightly beaten egg white and sprinkle lightly with some of the remaining 2 tablespoons of sugar. Repeat process with remaining 3 pastry strips, arranging cookies 2 inches apart on the cookie sheet.

5 Bake 20 minutes, until pastry is golden brown. Transfer letters to wire racks to cool completely. Repeat process with remaining pastry and filling. Makes 16.

PER 1/2 COOKIE		DAILY GOAL
Calories	140	2,000 (F), 2,500 (M)
Total Fat	8 g	60 g or less (F), 70 g or less (M)
Saturated fat	4 g	20 g or less (F), 23 g or less (M)
Cholesterol	29 mg	300 mg or less
Sodium	23 mg	2,400 mg or less
Carbohydrates	14 g	250 g or more
Protein	2 g	55 g to 90 g

NOTES

MANDELBROT

This firm cookie from Israel is perfect for dunking in coffee, tea, cocoa, or hot cider.

Prep time: 20 minutes plus cooling
Baking time: 39 to 44 minutes
O *Degree of difficulty: easy*
❄ *Can be frozen up to 3 months*

- 3 **cups all-purpose flour**
- 1 **teaspoon baking powder**
- 1 **teaspoon anise seeds, crushed**
- ½ **teaspoon grated lemon peel**
- ¼ **teaspoon salt**
- 1 **cup granulated sugar**
- 6 **tablespoons vegetable oil**
- 3 **large eggs**
- ½ **cup finely chopped walnuts *or* almonds**

1 Preheat oven to 350°F. Combine the flour, baking powder, anise seeds, lemon peel, and salt in a medium bowl. Beat the sugar, oil, and eggs in a large mixing bowl at high speed until pale and thick. Gradually beat in flour mixture at low speed until well blended. Stir in the walnuts.

2 Divide dough in half. With floured hands, shape each half into a 12x3-inch loaf. Place the loaves 3 inches apart on an ungreased cookie sheet. Bake 25 to 30 minutes, until lightly browned. Transfer the loaves to wire racks and cool 10 minutes; leave oven on.

3 Cut each log diagonally into ½-inch slices. Place cut side down on cookie sheets. Bake 7 minutes, until bottoms of cookies turn golden. Turn cookies over and bake 7 minutes more, until both sides are lightly toasted. Transfer the cookies to wire racks to cool completely. Makes 3 dozen.

PER COOKIE		DAILY GOAL
Calories	95	2,000 (F), 2,500 (M)
Total Fat	4 g	60 g or less (F), 70 g or less (M)
Saturated fat	.5 g	20 g or less (F), 23 g or less (M)
Cholesterol	18 mg	300 mg or less
Sodium	33 mg	2,400 mg or less
Carbohydrates	14 g	250 g or more
Protein	2 g	55 g to 90 g

NOTES

RUNNY-BUTTER TARTS

These Canadian charmers are bite-size cousins of the American chess pie or pecan pie.

Prep time: 35 minutes plus chilling
Baking time: 12 to 13 minutes
*   per batch*
Degree of difficulty: moderate
Can be frozen up to 1 month

2¼ **cups all-purpose flour**
¼   **teaspoon salt**
½   **cup cold butter, cut up**
      (no substitutions)
¼   **cup vegetable shortening**
4   **to 5 tablespoons ice water**
1   **large egg**
1   **tablespoon hot water**
1½ **teaspoons butter, melted**
      (no substitutions)
½   **teaspoon vanilla extract**
1   **cup firmly packed brown sugar**
½   **cup finely chopped walnuts**

1 Combine the flour and salt in a medium bowl. With pastry blender or 2 knives, cut in the butter and shortening until mixture resembles coarse crumbs. Sprinkle with ice water, 1 tablespoon at a time, tossing with a fork until pastry just holds together. Shape into a ball, then flatten into a disk. Wrap and refrigerate 1 hour or overnight.

2 Whisk together the egg, hot water, melted butter, vanilla, and brown sugar until smooth. Stir in the walnuts.

3 Preheat oven to 400°F. Divide pastry in half. On a lightly floured surface, roll one half ⅛ inch thick (keep remaining pastry refrigerated). Cut into circles with a 2¾-inch round cookie cutter. Gently press each circle into a 1¾-inch mini muffin pan cup.

4 Spoon 1 teaspoon filling into the pastry in each muffin cup. Bake 12 to 13 minutes, until tarts are golden brown. Carefully unmold the tarts and transfer to wire racks to cool completely. Repeat process with remaining pastry, rerolling scraps. Makes 4 dozen.

PER COOKIE		DAILY GOAL
Calories	75	2,000 (F), 2,500 (M)
Total Fat	4 g	60 g or less (F), 70 g or less (M)
Saturated fat	2 g	20 g or less (F), 23 g or less (M)
Cholesterol	10 mg	300 mg or less
Sodium	35 mg	2,400 mg or less
Carbohydrates	9 g	250 g or more
Protein	1 g	55 g to 90 g

NOTES

KOLACHKIS

These fabulous Czech walnut pastries were prize-winners in a Ladies' Home Journal heritage recipe contest. It is a family recipe from reader Marcia Brown.

Prep time: 1 hour 10 minutes
plus chilling
Baking time: 25 to 30 minutes
per batch
● *Degree of difficulty: moderate*
❄ *Can be frozen up to 3 months*

1 **package (8 ounces) cream cheese, cut up**
1 **cup butter *or* margarine, cut up**
1½ **teaspoons vanilla extract, divided**
2 **cups all-purpose flour**
1 **pound walnuts, finely ground**
6 **tablespoons butter *or* margarine, melted**
¼ **cup milk**
6 **tablespoons granulated sugar**
Confectioners' sugar

1 Combine the cream cheese, butter, and 1 teaspoon of the vanilla in a large bowl. With a pastry blender or 2 knives, cut in the flour, 1 cup at a time, until dough is thoroughly mixed. Shape into a ball, then flatten into a disk. Wrap and refrigerate overnight.

2 Combine the walnuts, melted butter, milk, granulated sugar, and the remaining ½ teaspoon vanilla in a large bowl.

3 Preheat oven to 350°F. Divide dough in half; keep one half refrigerated. Sprinkle work surface with confectioners' sugar. Roll one dough half into a 12x10-inch rectangle, adding confectioners' sugar as needed. Spread half the filling (1½ cups) evenly over dough. Cut dough into 2-inch squares and roll each square up jelly-roll fashion. Place the cookies seam side down 1 inch apart on ungreased cookie sheets.

4 Bake 25 to 30 minutes, until lightly browned on bottom. Transfer the cookies to wire racks to cool completely. Repeat process with remaining dough and filling. Sprinkle the tops of the cookies with additional confectioners' sugar. Makes 5 dozen.

PER COOKIE		DAILY GOAL
Calories	120	2,000 (F), 2,500 (M)
Total Fat	10 g	60 g or less (F), 70 g or less (M)
Saturated fat	4 g	20 g or less (F), 23 g or less (M)
Cholesterol	15 mg	300 mg or less
Sodium	55 mg	2,400 mg or less
Carbohydrates	6 g	250 g or more
Protein	2 g	55 g to 90 g

NOTES

CHINESE ALMOND COOKIES

Grown-ups will love the subtle flavor of these beauties, and kids will delight in rolling the dough into balls and placing the whole nuts on top.

Prep time: 20 minutes
Baking time: 10 to 12 minutes
    per batch
O   Degree of difficulty: easy
✳   Can be frozen up to 3 months

1¾ cups all-purpose flour
 1 teaspoon baking powder
 ½ teaspoon baking soda
 ⅛ teaspoon salt
 ½ cup lard *or* vegetable shortening
 ¾ cup granulated sugar
 1 large egg
 1 teaspoon almond extract
 ½ teaspoon vanilla extract
 1 large egg, lightly beaten
36 whole blanched almonds

1 Preheat oven to 350°F. Grease 2 cookie sheets. Combine the flour, baking powder, baking soda, and salt in a medium bowl. Beat the lard and sugar in a large mixing bowl at medium speed until light. Add the egg, beating until light and fluffy. Beat in the almond and vanilla extracts. Gradually beat in flour mixture at low speed until blended.

2 Roll dough into 1¼-inch balls. Arrange 2 inches apart on prepared cookie sheets. Flatten each ball slightly with palm of hand and brush lightly with beaten egg. Gently press an almond in the center of each cookie. Bake 10 to 12 minutes, until golden brown. Transfer the cookies to wire racks to cool completely. Makes 3 dozen.

PER COOKIE		DAILY GOAL
Calories	75	2,000 (F), 2,500 (M)
Total Fat	3 g	60 g or less (F), 70 g or less (M)
Saturated fat	1 g	20 g or less (F), 23 g or less (M)
Cholesterol	15 mg	300 mg or less
Sodium	37 mg	2,400 mg or less
Carbohydrates	9 g	250 g or more
Protein	1 g	55 g to 90 g

RUGELACH

The addition of yeast makes the dough easier to handle than in other versions of this crescent-shaped, cinnamon-nut cookie from Russia.

Prep time: 1 hour 20 minutes
*   plus chilling*
Baking time: 12 to 15 minutes
*   per batch*
Degree of difficulty: moderate
Can be frozen up to 3 months

1   **package active dry yeast**
½   **cups plus 2 tablespoons granulated sugar, divided**
½   **cup warm water (105°F.-115°F.)**
3   **cups all-purpose flour**
½   **teaspoon salt**
3   **large egg yolks**
½   **cup heavy *or* whipping cream**
1   **teaspoon vanilla extract**
1   **cup butter *or* margarine, softened**
2   **large egg whites, at room temperature**
¾   **cups toasted walnuts, finely chopped**
⅛   **teaspoon salt**
3   **tablespoons cinnamon**

1   Dissolve the yeast and 2 tablespoons of the sugar in warm water in a small bowl. Combine the flour and salt in a large mixing bowl. With a heavy-duty mixer at low speed, or by hand with a wooden spoon, beat in the yeast mixture, egg yolks, cream, and vanilla. Gradually beat in the butter, 2 tablespoons at a time, until blended. Wrap dough in plastic wrap and refrigerate several hours or overnight.

2   Meanwhile, for filling, beat egg whites to soft peaks in a small mixing bowl. Gently fold in the walnuts, ¾ cup of the remaining sugar, and salt with a rubber spatula.

3   Preheat oven to 350°F. Line 2 cookie sheets with foil; grease foil. Combine the remaining ¾ cup sugar and cinnamon in a small bowl, then sprinkle 1 heaping tablespoon of the mixture on a work surface. Divide dough into 10 pieces. Shape into balls. Refrigerate until ready to use.

4   Roll one ball into an 8-inch circle, turning to coat well with cinnamon-sugar. Cut the circle into 8 wedges with a long sharp knife. Place 1 level teaspoon of the walnut filling on the outer edge of each wedge. Roll wedges up from the outer

edge. Transfer the cookies to prepared cookie sheets, curving each cookie into a crescent shape. Repeat with remaining dough, cinnamon-sugar, and filling. Bake 12 to 15 minutes, until browned and puffed. Transfer the cookies to wire racks to cool completely. Makes 80.

PER COOKIE		DAILY GOAL
Calories	80	2,000 (F), 2,500 (M)
Total Fat	5 g	60 g or less (F), 70 g or less (M)
Saturated fat	2 g	20 g or less (F), 23 g or less (M)
Cholesterol	16 mg	300 mg or less
Sodium	44 mg	2,400 mg or less
Carbohydrates	8 g	250 g or more
Protein	1 g	55 g to 90 g

NOTES

93

BIZCOCHOS

New York chef Zarela Martinez shared these Mexican childhood favorites with us. Traditionally prepared with lard, a high fat shortening, these are super-flaky cookies. Be sure the lard has a fresh scent before using it and keep any unused portion refrigerated.

Prep time: 30 minutes plus chilling
Baking time: 6 to 7 minutes per batch
● *Degree of difficulty: moderate*
❄ *Can be frozen up to 3 months*

3¼ **cups all-purpose flour**
1½ **teaspoons baking powder**
¼ **teaspoon salt**
8 **ounces lard *or* 1 cup butter, softened**
⅔ **cup plus ½ cup granulated sugar, divided**
1 **large egg**
1½ **teaspoons grated orange peel**
1 **tablespoon cinnamon**

1 Combine the flour, baking powder, and salt in a medium bowl. Beat the lard in a mixing bowl until light and fluffy. Gradually beat in ⅔ cup of the sugar. Beat in the egg and orange peel. Gradually beat in flour mixture at low speed until combined. Cover and refrigerate until firm, 2 hours or overnight.

2 Preheat oven to 375°F. Divide dough in half. On a lightly floured surface, roll one half of dough ⅛ inch thick with a lightly floured rolling pin (keep remaining dough refrigerated). Cut into desired shapes with cookie cutters. Transfer the cookies to ungreased cookie sheets. Bake 6 to 7 minutes, until edges are golden. Transfer the cookies to wire racks.

3 Meanwhile, combine the remaining ½ cup sugar with the cinnamon and sprinkle over warm cookies. Cool completely. Repeat process with remaining dough. Makes 6 dozen.

PER COOKIE		DAILY GOAL
Calories	65	2,000 (F), 2,500 (M)
Total Fat	3 g	60 g or less (F), 70 g or less (M)
Saturated fat	1 g	20 g or less (F), 23 g or less (M)
Cholesterol	6 mg	300 mg or less
Sodium	17 mg	2,400 mg or less
Carbohydrates	8 g	250 g or more
Protein	1 g	55 g to 90 g

WEDDING CAKES

A universal favorite, also known as Mexican wedding cakes or Russian tea cakes, these nutty morsels are melt-in-your-mouth crowd pleasers. If you prefer, use ground almonds instead of the pecans.

Prep time: 20 minutes
Baking time: 25 minutes per batch
Degree of difficulty: easy
✳ *Can be frozen up to 3 months*

1 **cup pecans**
2 **cups all-purpose flour**
½ **cup sifted confectioners' sugar**
   Pinch salt
1 **teaspoon vanilla extract**
1 **cup butter, softened and cut up**
   (no substitutions)
   Additional sifted confectioners'
   sugar, for decoration

1 Preheat oven to 325°F. Spread the pecans on a baking sheet in a single layer. Bake 10 minutes, until lightly browned and fragrant. Cool the nuts completely and then finely chop. Leave oven on.

2 Combine the chopped pecans, flour, confectioners' sugar, and salt in a large bowl. Stir in the vanilla. With pastry blender or 2 knives, cut in the butter until mixture resembles fine crumbs. Gently knead dough until it begins to hold together.

3 Roll dough into ¾-inch balls and arrange 1½ inches apart on ungreased cookie sheets. Bake 25 minutes, until lightly browned. Transfer the cookies to wire racks and cool slightly, 5 minutes. Roll cookies in additional sifted confectioners' sugar and cool completely. Roll in additional confectioners' sugar before serving. Makes 4½ dozen.

PER COOKIE		DAILY GOAL
Calories	65	2,000 (F), 2,500 (M)
Total Fat	5 g	60 g or less (F), 70 g or less (M)
Saturated fat	2 g	20 g or less (F), 23 g or less (M)
Cholesterol	9 mg	300 mg or less
Sodium	37 mg	2,400 mg or less
Carbohydrates	5 g	250 g or more
Protein	1 g	55 g to 90 g

COOKIES FOR

CHRISTMAS

'Tis the season for cookies—
cookies of whimsical shapes,
piped icing, and colored sugars.
'Tis the season when baking is a
family tradition and sharing the
bounty is a special joy. Here, we
share with you the special
cookies from our Christmas
kitchen. This chapter brims with
such favorite recipes as Spiced
Gingerbread Men, Tiny
Fruitcakes, and shortbread
Candy Cane Twists.

HOLIDAY MARZIPAN BARS

Here's a bar cookie perfect for Christmas. It's triple layered with a buttery pale-green marzipan filling, peach preserves, and a chocolate glaze. The bars can be refrigerated up to 2 days ahead and ready in a jiffy when company comes to call.

Prep time: 30 minutes
Baking time: 45 to 50 minutes
● *Degree of difficulty: moderate*

2¼ **cups butter, softened (no substitutions), divided**
1½ **cups granulated sugar, divided**
1 **large egg yolk**
3¼ **cups all-purpose flour, divided**
1 **tube (7 ounces) *or* 1 can (8 ounces) almond paste**
5 **large eggs**
1 **teaspoon vanilla extract**
6 **drops green food coloring**
2 **tablespoons cornstarch**
½ **cup peach preserves**
4 **squares (4 ounces) semisweet chocolate, coarsely chopped**

1 Preheat oven to 375°F. Beat 1 cup of the butter and ½ cup of the sugar in a large mixing bowl at medium speed until light. Beat in the egg yolk until light and fluffy. Gradually beat in 2½ cups of the flour at low speed just until combined. With lightly floured fingertips, press dough evenly in a 15½x10½-inch jelly-roll pan. Bake 20 minutes, until golden. Cool on a wire rack 5 minutes.

2 Meanwhile, beat the remaining 1¼ cups butter, the remaining 1 cup sugar, and almond paste in a clean large mixing bowl at medium speed until light and fluffy. Beat in the eggs, one at a time, beating well after each addition. Beat in the vanilla and green food coloring. Combine the remaining ¾ cup flour and the cornstarch in a small bowl; fold into almond paste mixture with a rubber spatula.

3 Spread the peach preserves over the crust, then spoon the marzipan mixture evenly over preserves. Bake 25 to 30 minutes, until golden. Cool completely in the pan on a wire rack.

4 Melt the chocolate in the top of a double boiler over simmering water. Spread chocolate evenly over marzipan layer.

Refrigerate bars 1 hour, until chocolate is set. Cut into 1½-inch squares. Makes 5½ dozen.

PER COOKIE		DAILY GOAL	
Calories	130	2,000 (F), 2,500 (M)	
Total Fat	8 g	60 g or less (F), 70 g or less (M)	
Saturated fat	4 g	20 g or less (F), 23 g or less (M)	
Cholesterol	36 mg	300 mg or less	
Sodium	70 mg	2,400 mg or less	
Carbohydrates	14 g	250 g or more	
Protein	2 g	55 g to 90 g	

NOTES

SOUR CREAM-
PECAN HORNS

Extra flaky, thanks to a delicate yeast dough, these fancy pastries are made for the holiday cookie tray. The nutty meringue filling can feature ground pecans or walnuts.

Prep time: 1 hour plus chilling
Baking time: 10 to 12 minutes
  per batch
Degree of difficulty: moderate
Can be frozen up to 3 months

 2 **cups all-purpose flour**
 ¾ **cup granulated sugar, divided**
 1 **teaspoon baking powder**
 ¼ **teaspoon salt**
 ½ **cup cold butter, cut up**
   (no substitutions)
 1½ **teaspoons active dry yeast**
 2 **tablespoons warm water**
   (105°F.-115°F.)
 2 **large eggs, separated**
 ¼ **cup sour cream**
 1 **teaspoon vanilla extract**
 ½ **cup finely ground pecans**
   or **walnuts**
 ½ **teaspoon almond extract**
 2 **tablespoons heavy** *or* **whipping**
   cream
   Decorative sugar, optional

1 Combine the flour, ¼ cup of the sugar, baking powder, and salt in a large bowl. With a pastry blender or 2 knives, cut in the butter until the mixture resembles coarse crumbs.

2 Dissolve the yeast in warm water in a small bowl; let stand 5 minutes until foamy. Whisk in the egg yolks, sour cream, and vanilla. Stir into dry ingredients until combined. Cover and refrigerate 1 hour or overnight.

3 Preheat oven to 350°F. Grease 2 cookie sheets. Beat the egg whites in a medium mixing bowl until foamy. Gradually beat in the remaining ½ cup sugar and beat to stiff peaks. Fold in the ground nuts and almond extract with a rubber spatula.

4 Divide dough into quarters. On a floured surface with a floured rolling pin, roll one quarter of the dough into a 9-inch circle (keep remaining dough refrigerated). Cut into 12 wedges. Spread 1 heaping teaspoon of the meringue on each. Roll up from wide end. Place rolls 2 inches apart on prepared cookie sheets. Brush lightly with the cream and sprinkle with decorative sugar. Bake 10 to 12 minutes, until just golden. Transfer the cookies to wire racks to cool completely. Makes 4 dozen.

PER COOKIE		DAILY GOAL
Calories	65	2,000 (F), 2,500 (M)
Total Fat	3.5 g	60 g or less (F), 70 g or less (M)
Saturated fat	2 g	20 g or less (F), 23 g or less (M)
Cholesterol	16 mg	300 mg or less
Sodium	46 mg	2,400 mg or less
Carbohydrates	7 g	250 g or more
Protein	1 g	55 g to 90 g

NOTES

BERLINERKRANSER

These butter twist cookies are a holiday favorite from Norway, but are also served throughout Scandanavia. *Also pictured on page 96.*

Prep time: 1 hour plus chilling
Baking time: 8 to 10 minutes
*   per batch*
Degree of difficulty: moderate
✳ *Can be frozen up to 3 months*

4 **large egg yolks**
¾ **cup confectioners' sugar**
1 **cup butter, softened**
    (no substitutions)
2 **cups all-purpose flour**
1 **large egg white, lightly beaten**
¼ **cup crushed, sugar cubes** *or*
    decorative sugar
    Red and green candied
    cherries, slivered

1 Beat the egg yolks and confectioners' sugar in a large mixing bowl at medium speed until light and fluffy. Add the butter, one tablespoon at a time, beating well after each addition. Gradually beat in the flour at low speed just until blended. Wrap and refrigerate 3 hours or overnight.

2 Preheat oven to 350°F. Grease 2 cookie sheets. Divide dough into quarters. Cut each quarter into 16 equal pieces (keep remaining dough refrigerated). On a lightly floured surface, roll each piece into a 5-inch-long rope. Place ropes on prepared cookie sheets and carefully twist each to form a loop, with ½ inch extending at both ends. Brush the cookies with the egg white and sprinkle on crushed or decorative sugar. Garnish with candied cherries. Bake 8 to 10 minutes, until golden. Transfer the cookies to wire racks to cool completely. Repeat with remaining dough. Makes 64.

PER COOKIE		DAILY GOAL
Calories	55	2,000 (F), 2,500 (M)
Total Fat	3 g	60 g or less (F), 70 g or less (M)
Saturated fat	2 g	20 g or less (F), 23 g or less (M)
Cholesterol	21 mg	300 mg or less
Sodium	32 mg	2,400 mg or less
Carbohydrates	5 g	250 g or more
Protein	0 g	55 g to 90 g

NOTES

101

CHERRY PINWHEELS

Here's a lovely snowflake-shaped cookie with a difference—creamed cottage cheese in the buttery dough! Our favorite is cherry-filled, but any good-quality preserves work well too.

Prep time: 1 hour plus chilling
Baking time: 12 to 15 minutes
*   per batch*
◑ *Degree of difficulty: moderate*
❄ *Can be frozen up to 1 month*

1 **container (8 ounces) creamed (4% fat) cottage cheese**
2 **cups all-purpose flour**
1 **cup cold butter, cut up (no substitutions)**
½ **cup premium sour-cherry *or* raspberry preserves**
1 **large egg white, lightly beaten**
⅓ **cup decorative pearl sugar *or* crushed sugar cubes**

1 Combine the cottage cheese and flour in a large bowl. With a pastry blender or 2 knives, cut in the butter until mixture resembles coarse crumbs. Press dough together then flatten into a thick disk. Divide dough into quarters. Wrap and refrigerate 4 hours or overnight.

2 Grease 2 cookie sheets. Roll 1 dough quarter ¹⁄₁₆ inch thick between 2 sheets of floured wax paper (keep remaining dough refrigerated). With a sharp knife, cut into 2½-inch squares. Transfer the dough squares to prepared cookie sheets. (If dough becomes too soft, refrigerate for a few minutes.)

3 Make a 1-inch diagonal cut from each corner toward the center of each square. Place ¼ teaspoon jam in center. Fold every other tip to the center over the jam to form a pinwheel. Refrigerate 10 minutes.

4 Preheat oven to 350°F. Lightly brush tops of dough with egg white and sprinkle with decorative sugar. Bake 12 to 15 minutes, until golden brown. Sprinkle with more sugar, if desired. Transfer to wire racks to cool completely. Makes 4½ dozen.

PER COOKIE		DAILY GOAL
Calories	65	2,000 (F), 2,500 (M)
Total Fat	4 g	60 g or less (F), 70 g or less (M)
Saturated fat	2 g	20 g or less (F), 23 g or less (M)
Cholesterol	10 mg	300 mg or less
Sodium	55 mg	2,400 mg or less
Carbohydrates	7 g	250 g or more
Protein	1 g	55 g to 90 g

CANDY CANE TWISTS

Pretty enough to hang on the tree, these buttery cookies are as much fun to make as they are to eat. Be sure the dough is chilled before forming it into twists.

Prep time: 35 minutes plus chilling
Baking time: 8 to 10 minutes
*   per batch*
Degree of difficulty: moderate
Can be frozen up to 1 month

2½ **cups all-purpose flour**
    Pinch salt
1   **cup butter, softened**
        (no substitutions)
¾   **cup granulated sugar**
1   **large egg**
1   **teaspoon peppermint extract**
½   **teaspoon vanilla extract**
¼   **teaspoon red food coloring**

1 Combine the flour and salt in a medium bowl. Beat the butter and sugar in a large mixing bowl at medium speed until light and fluffy. Beat in the egg, peppermint, and vanilla extracts. Divide dough in half. Blend the red coloring into half of dough. Cover dough halves separately and refrigerate 30 minutes.

2 Preheat oven to 350°F. For each cookie, roll 1 scant tablespoon each white and red dough into 6-inch-long ropes. Place ropes side by side, press lightly together and twist. Arrange the cookies on an ungreased cookie sheet and curve one end to form each cane handle. Repeat with remaining dough.

3 Bake cookies 8 to 10 minutes, until edges are golden. Transfer the cookies to wire racks to cool completely. Makes 4 dozen.

PER COOKIE		DAILY GOAL
Calories	70	2,000 (F), 2,500 (M)
Total Fat	4 g	60 g or less (F), 70 g or less (M)
Saturated fat	2 g	20 g or less (F), 23 g or less (M)
Cholesterol	15 mg	300 mg or less
Sodium	43 mg	2,400 mg or less
Carbohydrates	8 g	250 g or more
Protein	1 g	55 g to 90 g

CLASSIC SPRITZ

These wonderful pressed cookies need only a sprinkle of decorative colored sugar.

Prep time: 30 minutes
Baking time: 8 to 10 minutes
*   per batch*
● *Degree of difficulty: moderate*
❆ *Can be frozen up to 1 month*

2   **cups all-purpose flour**
½   **teaspoon baking powder**
¼   **teaspoon salt**
1   **cup butter, softened**
        (no substitutions)
¾   **cup granulated sugar**
1   **large egg**
½   **teaspoon almond extract** *or*
        1 teaspoon vanilla extract
    Decorative sugar

1 Preheat oven to 375°F. Combine the flour, baking powder and salt in a small bowl. Beat the butter and sugar in a large mixing bowl at medium speed until light and fluffy. Beat in the egg and almond extract. Gradually beat in flour mixture at low speed just until combined.

2 Attach desired template to the cookie press. Fill the press with half the dough and press cookies about 2 inches apart onto ungreased cookie sheets. Sprinkle with decorative sugar. Bake 8 to 10 minutes, just until edges are lightly golden. Transfer the cookies to wire racks to cool completely. Repeat with remaining dough. Makes 6½ dozen.

PER COOKIE		DAILY GOAL
Calories	40	2,000 (F), 2,500 (M)
Total Fat	2 g	60 g or less (F), 70 g or less (M)
Saturated fat	1 g	20 g or less (F), 23 g or less (M)
Cholesterol	9 mg	300 mg or less
Sodium	35 mg	2,400 mg or less
Carbohydrates	4 g	250 g or more
Protein	0 g	55 g to 90 g

HOT OFF THE PRESS: SPRITZ AND OTHER MOLDED COOKIES

A cookie press or a cookie gun, which includes a selection of decorative templates, is a handy tool to create easy molded cookies. A soft, buttery dough is spooned into the press, then pushed through the template to form a design. When filling the press, only spoon in a half of the dough at a time and be sure to press the cookies on a completely cooled cookie sheet.

NOTES

MERINGUE MUSHROOMS

For gift giving, place a few meringues in a produce basket and wrap with colored cellophane.

Prep time: 45 minutes
Baking time: 2 hours
● *Degree of difficulty: moderate*

4   **large egg whites, at room temperature**
¼   **teaspoon cream of tartar**
⅛   **teaspoon salt**
1   **cup granulated sugar**
1   **teaspoon vanilla extract**
6   **squares (6 ounces) semisweet chocolate, coarsely chopped**
   Unsweetened cocoa powder, for decoration

1 Preheat oven to 225°F. Line 2 cookie sheets with foil. Beat the egg whites, cream of tartar, and salt in a large mixing bowl at medium speed until frothy. Gradually increasing speed to high, add sugar, 2 tablespoons at a time. Add vanilla. Beat until the sugar is dissolved and stiff peaks form, 5 minutes.

2 For stems, spoon the meringue into a large pastry bag with a ½-inch-round tip. Holding the tip vertically and close to one foil-lined cookie sheet, press gently while slowly raising bag straight up. Cut the stem from tip with a small knife. Make forty-eight 1- to 1½-inch stems.

3 For caps, keeping tip close to the other foil-lined cookie sheet, hold the bag vertically and press to form 48 meringue mounds, each 1½ inches wide. Smooth the tops of the caps with moist fingertip.

4 Bake the meringue stems and caps 2 hours. Turn oven off and cool the meringues completely in oven.

5 To assemble the mushrooms, melt the chocolate in a double boiler over hot, not boiling, water until smooth. Remove from heat and cool slightly. Gently peel meringue stems and caps from foil. Spread

½ teaspoon melted chocolate on the underside of a cap and attach a stem. Let set in a cool, dry place before turning upright. (Can be made ahead. Store in airtight containers up to 2 days. Do not freeze.) Before serving, lightly sprinkle mushroom tops with cocoa. Makes 4 dozen.

PER COOKIE		DAILY GOAL
Calories	35	2,000 (F), 2,500 (M)
Total Fat	1 g	60 g or less (F), 70 g or less (M)
Saturated fat	1 g	20 g or less (F), 23 g or less (M)
Cholesterol	0 mg	300 mg or less
Sodium	10 mg	2,400 mg or less
Carbohydrates	6 g	250 g or more
Protein	0 g	55 g to 90 g

NOTES

PEPPERMINT KISSES

Crushed peppermint candies add just the right amount of sparkle to these crisp meringue cookies.

▼ *Low-fat*
▽ *Low-calorie*
  Prep time: 30 minutes plus cooling
  Baking time: 1 hour 15 minutes
◯ *Degree of difficulty: easy*

  2 **large egg whites, at room temperature**
 ¼ **teaspoon cream of tartar**
 ⅛ **teaspoon salt**
 ½ **cup granulated sugar**
 ½ **teaspoon vanilla extract**
  1 **drop red food coloring**
 ½ **cup crushed peppermint candy**

1 Preheat oven to 225°F. Line 2 cookie sheets with foil.

2 Beat the egg whites in a large mixing bowl at medium speed until foamy. Add the cream of tartar and salt and continue to beat until soft peaks form. Gradually beat in the sugar, one tablespoon at a time, then continue to beat until stiff. Beat in the vanilla and food coloring. Gently fold the peppermint candy into whites with a rubber spatula just until blended.

3 Spoon the meringue into a large pastry bag fitted with a ½-inch star tip. Pipe kisses onto prepared cookie sheets. Bake 1 hour 15 minutes. Turn oven off. Cool in oven at least 1 hour 30 minutes or overnight. Carefully remove from foil. Makes 4 dozen.

PER COOKIE		DAILY GOAL
Calories	15	2,000 (F), 2,500 (M)
Total Fat	0 g	60 g or less (F), 70 g or less (M)
Saturated fat	0 g	20 g or less (F), 23 g or less (M)
Cholesterol	0 mg	300 mg or less
Sodium	8 mg	2,400 mg or less
Carbohydrates	3 g	250 g or more
Protein	0 g	55 g to 90 g

WHITE CHRISTMAS COOKIES

This all-time favorite was given to us by the New York Restaurant School in New York City.

Prep time: 15 minutes
Baking time: 8 to 10 minutes
* per batch*
○ *Degree of difficulty: easy*
❇ *Can be frozen up to 1 month*

2¼ **cups all-purpose flour**
 1 **teaspoon baking soda**
 1 **teaspoon salt**
 1 **cup unsalted butter, softened**
     (no substitutions)
 ¾ **cup firmly packed brown sugar**
 ¾ **cup granulated sugar**
 3 **large eggs**
 1 **teaspoon vanilla extract**
12 **ounces white chocolate, coarsely**
     chopped
 ¾ **cup coarsely chopped salted**
     macadamia nuts
1¼ **cups golden raisins**
     Confectioners' sugar, for
     decoration

1 Preheat oven to 350°F. Lightly grease 2 cookie sheets.

2 Combine the flour, baking soda, and salt in a medium bowl. Beat the butter, brown sugar, and granulated sugar in a large mixing bowl at medium speed until light and fluffy. Add the eggs, one at a time, beating well after each addition. Beat in the vanilla. Beat in flour mixture at low speed until blended. Stir in the white chocolate, macadamia nuts, and raisins.

3 Drop dough by rounded teaspoonfuls onto prepared cookie sheets. Bake 8 to 10 minutes, until pale golden. Transfer the cookies to wire racks to cool completely. Sift confectioners' sugar over the tops of cookies before serving. Makes 6 dozen.

PER COOKIE		DAILY GOAL
Calories	100	2,000 (F), 2,500 (M)
Total Fat	5 g	60 g or less (F), 70 g or less (M)
Saturated fat	3 g	20 g or less (F), 23 g or less (M)
Cholesterol	16 mg	300 mg or less
Sodium	58 mg	2,400 mg or less
Carbohydrates	12 g	250 g or more
Protein	1 g	55 g to 90 g

NOTES

108

GINGER-LACE COOKIES

These ultra-thin, crunchy cookies, spiced with fresh ginger, get their lacy texture from melted butter, light corn syrup, and molasses. They can be prepared up to 3 days ahead and stored in an airtight container at room temperature.

Prep time: 20 minutes
Baking time: 7 to 10 minutes
   per batch
Degree of difficulty: moderate

½ **cup butter, cut up**
      (no substitutions)
6 **tablespoons light corn syrup**
3 **tablespoons granulated sugar**
2 **tablespoons light molasses**
⅔ **cup all-purpose flour**
1 **tablespoon grated fresh ginger**
½ **teaspoon vanilla extract**

1 Preheat oven to 350°F. Line 3 cookie sheets with foil.

2 Bring the butter, syrup, sugar, and molasses to a boil in a large saucepan over medium-high heat. Remove from heat. Sift in the flour and whisk until smooth. Whisk in the ginger and vanilla. Place the pan in a larger pan of hot water to keep batter warm.

3 Drop the batter by teaspoonfuls onto prepared cookie sheets (12 per sheet). Bake 7 to 10 minutes, until brown. Cool cookies on cookie sheet 2 minutes, then transfer them, with the foil, to wire racks. Let the cookies stand until firm enough to remove from foil. Cool completely on racks. Makes 3 dozen.

PER COOKIE		DAILY GOAL
Calories	50	2,000 (F), 2,500 (M)
Total Fat	3 g	60 g or less (F), 70 g or less (M)
Saturated fat	2 g	20 g or less (F), 23 g or less (M)
Cholesterol	7 mg	300 mg or less
Sodium	31 mg	2,400 mg or less
Carbohydrates	6 g	250 g or more
Protein	0 g	55 g to 90 g

TINY FRUITCAKES

Here's a bite-sized version of fruitcake that will become a favorite for all those gathered round the Christmas tree. Not overly sweet, these festive miniatures feature an assortment of dried fruits, including dried cranberries.

Prep time: 25 minutes
Baking time: 25 to 30 minutes per batch
Degree of difficulty: easy

- 1 **cup currants** *or* **chopped raisins**
- ½ **cup finely chopped dried figs**
  Boiling water
- 1 **cup dried cranberries**
- ½ **cup finely chopped dried pineapple**
- ¼ **cup dark rum**
- 1 **cup all-purpose flour**
- 1 **teaspoon cinnamon**
- ½ **teaspoon baking powder**
- ¼ **teaspoon salt**
- ¼ **teaspoon nutmeg**
- ¼ **teaspoon cloves**
- ½ **cup butter** *or* **margarine, softened**
- 1 **cup firmly packed brown sugar**
- 1 **large egg**
- 1 **teaspoon grated orange peel**
- 1 **cup finely chopped pecans**
- ¼ **cup apricot preserves, optional**
- 60 **pecan halves, optional**

1 Preheat oven to 350°F. Line miniature muffin-pan cups with paper or foil liners.

2 Combine the currants and figs in a medium bowl with just enough boiling water to cover. Let stand 5 minutes, then drain well. Return to bowl with the cranberries, pineapple, and rum. Let the fruit mixture stand at least 10 minutes, stirring occasionally.

3 Meanwhile, combine the flour, cinnamon, baking powder, salt, nutmeg, and cloves in a small bowl. Beat the butter in a large mixing bowl at medium speed until creamy. Beat in the brown sugar until light and fluffy. Beat in the egg, then the orange peel. Beat in dry ingredients until well combined. Stir in fruit-rum mixture, and chopped pecans.

4 Spoon by heaping teaspoonfuls into prepared muffin-pan cups. Bake 25 to 30 minutes, until a toothpick inserted in one fruitcake comes out clean. Cool fruitcakes in pan 5 minutes. Remove from pan and cool completely on wire racks. Repeat baking remaining batter.

5 If desired, heat the apricot preserves in a small saucepan over medium heat. Bring just to a boil. Remove from heat and brush the tops of fruitcakes with warm preserves and garnish each with 1 pecan half. Store in a single layer in tightly covered containers up to 3 weeks. Makes 5 dozen.

PER COOKIE		DAILY GOAL
Calories	75	2,000 (F), 2,500 (M)
Total Fat	3 g	60 g or less (F), 70 g or less (M)
Saturated fat	1 g	20 g or less (F), 23 g or less (M)
Cholesterol	8 mg	300 mg or less
Sodium	34 mg	2,400 mg or less
Carbohydrates	12 g	250 g or more
Protein	1 g	55 g to 90 g

NOTES

111

MOCHA-HAZELNUT DROPS

These festive chocolate morsels, flavored with a touch of coffee, are topped off with a bright candied cherry.

Prep time: 40 minutes plus chilling
Baking time: 8 to 10 minutes
*   per batch*
O *Degree of difficulty: easy*
❄ *Can be frozen up to 1 month*

1¼ **cups hazelnuts**
1 **cup all-purpose flour**
¼ **cup unsweetened cocoa powder**
1 **teaspoon baking powder**
¼ **teaspoon salt**
½ **cup butter *or* margarine, softened**
1 **cup granulated sugar**
1 **teaspoon instant coffee powder**
2 **teaspoons hot water**
1 **large egg**
½ **teaspoon vanilla extract**
30 **candied cherries, halved**

1 Preheat oven to 350°F. Spread the hazelnuts on a baking sheet in a single layer. Bake 12 to 15 minutes, until lightly browned and skins are crackly. Wrap nuts in a clean kitchen towel and let stand 5 minutes. Rub the nuts in the towel to remove skins, then cool completely. Place the nuts in a food processor and process until finely chopped. Leave oven on.

2 Grease 2 cookie sheets. Combine the flour, cocoa, baking powder, and salt in a medium bowl. Beat the butter in a large mixing bowl at medium speed until smooth. Gradually beat in the sugar until light and fluffy. Dissolve the coffee in hot water and add it to creamed butter-sugar mixture. Beat in the egg and vanilla until blended. Beat in flour mixture at low speed just until combined. Refrigerate dough 15 minutes.

3 Roll dough into 1-inch balls. Roll each ball in chopped hazelnuts. Place 2 inches apart on prepared cookie sheets. Lightly press the tops to flatten, then press 1 candied cherry half onto each cookie. Bake 8 to 10 minutes. Transfer the cookies to wire racks to cool completely. Makes 5 dozen.

PER COOKIE		DAILY GOAL
Calories	60	2,000 (F), 2,500 (M)
Total Fat	3 g	60 g or less (F), 70 g or less (M)
Saturated fat	1 g	20 g or less (F), 23 g or less (M)
Cholesterol	8 mg	300 mg or less
Sodium	36 mg	2,400 mg or less
Carbohydrates	8 g	250 g or more
Protein	1 g	55 g to 90 g

NOTES

AUNTIE MARY'S COOKIES

These cookies are served each Christmas in the home of our Associate Food Editor Susan Westmoreland, thanks to her Aunt Mary.

Prep time: 15 minutes plus chilling
Baking time: 20 minutes per batch
Degree of difficulty: moderate

2   **cups all-purpose flour**
½   **teaspoon baking powder**
¼   **teaspoon salt**
½   **cup butter *or* margarine, softened**
1   **package (3 ounces) cream cheese, softened**
½   **cup granulated sugar**
½   **cup firmly packed brown sugar**
1   **large egg**
1   **teaspoon vanilla extract**
⅔   **cup sweetened condensed milk**
⅔   **cup (4 ounces) semisweet chocolate chips**
½   **cup chopped walnuts**
    Confectioners' sugar, for garnish

1 Combine the flour, baking powder, and salt in a medium bowl. Beat the butter, cream cheese, granulated sugar, and brown sugar in a large mixing bowl at medium speed until light and fluffy. Add the egg and vanilla and beat until well blended. Beat in flour mixture at low speed just until combined. Divide dough in quarters. Wrap each piece and refrigerate 2 hours or overnight.

2 Combine the condensed milk and chocolate in a medium saucepan and cook over medium heat until chocolate is melted. Remove from heat and stir in the walnuts. Cool to room temperature.

3 Preheat oven to 350°F. Grease 2 cookie sheets. Roll each dough quarter on a well floured surface into a 10x6-inch rectangle. Spread one quarter of the filling lengthwise down the center of each rectangle. Fold the dough lengthwise in thirds over filling. With a metal spatula, transfer rolls seam side down to cookie sheets.

4 Bake 20 minutes, until lightly browned. Transfer the rolls to wire racks and cool completely. Sprinkle each roll with confectioners' sugar and cut into 12 triangles. Makes 4 dozen.

PER COOKIE		DAILY GOAL
Calories	95	2,000 (F), 2,500 (M)
Total Fat	5 g	60 g or less (F), 70 g or less (M)
Saturated fat	2 g	20 g or less (F), 23 g or less (M)
Cholesterol	13 mg	300 mg or less
Sodium	51 mg	2,400 mg or less
Carbohydrates	12 g	250 g or more
Protein	1 g	55 g to 90 g

NOTES

SUGAR CUT-OUTS

Here are the classic, snowy-white sugar cookies for the holidays. They're simply lovely plain, but we've included two special ways to finish and decorate them.

Prep time: 1 hour plus chilling
Baking time: 8 to 9 minutes per batch
⬤ *Degree of difficulty: moderate*
❄ *Can be frozen up to 1 month*

2½ **cups all-purpose flour**
¼ **teaspoon salt**
1 **cup butter, softened**
   (no substitutions)
1 **cup granulated sugar**
1 **large egg**
1½ **teaspoons grated lemon peel**
½ **teaspoon vanilla extract**

Confectioners' Icing
2 **cups confectioners' sugar**
5 **to 7 teaspoons milk**

1 Combine the flour and salt in a medium bowl. Beat the butter and sugar in a large mixing bowl at medium speed until light and fluffy. Add the egg, lemon peel,

and vanilla and beat until blended. Beat in flour mixture at low speed just until combined. Divide dough into quarters. Wrap each piece and refrigerate overnight.

2 Preheat oven to 350°F. Grease 4 cookie sheets. Between 2 sheets of lightly floured wax paper, roll one dough quarter ⅛ inch thick (keep remaining dough refrigerated). Remove wax paper and cut with floured 2- to 3-inch cookie cutters into desired shapes. Transfer cut-outs to prepared cookie sheets. Bake 8 to 9 minutes, until edges are golden. Transfer the cookies to wire racks to cool completely. Repeat rolling and cutting remaining dough, rerolling scraps. Decorate with Confectioners' Icing as desired. Makes 7 dozen.

Confectioners' Icing: Place the confectioners' sugar in a small mixing bowl. Stir in enough of the milk to make the icing smooth and spreadable. Color as desired (see tip, at right). Makes ¾ cup.

PER COOKIE		DAILY GOAL
Calories	45	2,000 (F), 2,500 (M)
Total Fat	2 g	60 g or less (F), 70 g or less (M)
Saturated fat	1 g	20 g or less (F), 23 g or less (M)
Cholesterol	8 mg	300 mg or less
Sodium	32 mg	2,400 mg or less
Carbohydrates	5 g	250 g or more
Protein	1 g	55 g to 90 g

ALL ABOUT ICING: DECORATING COOKIES

Whether you pipe it or spread it, icing is a great way to dress up any cookie recipe. Follow the hints below for coloring and piping icing.

• To use liquid coloring, add the color, one drop at a time, stirring after each addition, until you reach the desired color. Cover surface of icing with plastic wrap until ready to use.

• To use a paste coloring, use a toothpick to remove a tiny portion of paste, then stir the coloring into icing. To achieve a deeper color, continue to add coloring in very small amounts.

• To pipe icing, use a clean pastry bag and tip for each color and practice on a piece of wax paper. If you don't have a pastry bag, use a heavy-duty plastic food storage bag with a zipper-top. Snip a tiny bit from one corner and twist the top of the bag to push the icing through the small opening.

LEBKUCHEN BEARS

These adorable little bears are a whimsical variation of the classic German holiday cookie flavored with candied fruit and honey.

Prep time: 45 minutes plus chilling
Baking time: 8 to 10 minutes
*   per batch*
● *Degree of difficulty: moderate*
❄ *Can be frozen up to 1 month*

2¾ **cups all-purpose flour**
2 **teaspoons cinnamon**
1 **teaspoon ginger**
1 **teaspoon baking soda**
¼ **teaspoon nutmeg**
¼ **teaspoon cloves**
¼ **teaspoon salt**
⅓ **cup finely chopped candied citron**
¾ **cup butter *or* margarine**
½ **cup granulated sugar**
½ **cup honey**
1 **large egg, lightly beaten**
    Confectioners' Icing (recipe
        page 114)

1 Combine the flour, cinnamon, ginger, baking soda, nutmeg, cloves, and salt in a medium bowl. Stir in the citron.

2 Heat the butter, sugar, and honey in a medium saucepan over medium heat until butter is melted. Remove from heat. Pour the melted butter mixture into flour mixture and stir until evenly moistened. Add the egg and stir until smooth. Let stand 10 minutes.

3 Divide dough in half. While still warm, between 2 sheets of wax paper, roll each half of dough ⅛ inch thick. Refrigerate on cookie sheets at least 1 hour or overnight.

4 Preheat oven to 350°F. Grease 2 cookie sheets. Remove wax paper and cut dough with a floured 3½-inch bear-shaped cookie cutter. Transfer cut-outs to prepared cookie sheets. Bake 8 to 10 minutes. Transfer the cookies to wire racks to cool completely. Reroll scraps and refrigerate; repeat cutting and baking. Decorate with Confectioners' Icing as desired. Makes 5 dozen.

PER COOKIE		DAILY GOAL
Calories	60	2,000 (F), 2,500 (M)
Total Fat	2 g	60 g or less (F), 70 g or less (M)
Saturated fat	1 g	20 g or less (F), 23 g or less (M)
Cholesterol	10 mg	300 mg or less
Sodium	60 mg	2,400 mg or less
Carbohydrates	9 g	250 g or more
Protein	1 g	55 g to 90 g

NOTES

PEPPARKAKOR

These delicate spice cookies from Scandanavia have a touch of orange peel. Use animal-shaped cookie cutters and watch the kids gobble them up.

Prep time: 1 hour plus chilling
Baking time: 8 to 10 minutes
  per batch
Degree of difficulty: moderate
Can be frozen up to 3 months

3¼ cups all-purpose flour
2 teaspoons baking soda
2 teaspoons cinnamon
½ teaspoon cloves
1 cup butter *or* margarine, softened
1½ cups granulated sugar
1 large egg
2 teaspoons grated orange peel
2 tablespoons dark corn syrup
  **Confectioners' Icing (recipe
    page 114)**

1 Combine the flour, baking soda, cinnamon, and cloves in a medium bowl. Beat the butter and sugar in a large mixing bowl at medium speed until light. Beat in the egg until light and fluffy. Add the orange peel and corn syrup and beat well. Beat in flour mixture at low speed until combined. Wrap dough and refrigerate overnight.

2 Preheat oven to 375°F. Divide dough into quarters. Between 2 sheets of lightly floured wax paper, roll one dough quarter ⅛ inch thick (keep remaining dough refrigerated). Remove wax paper and cut dough into desired shapes with floured 3-inch cookie cutters.

3 Transfer cut-outs to ungreased cookie sheets. Bake 8 to 10 minutes. Transfer the cookies to wire racks to cool completely. Repeat rolling and cutting remaining dough, rerolling scraps. Decorate with Confectioners' Icing as desired. Makes 6 dozen.

PER COOKIE		DAILY GOAL
Calories	60	2,000 (F), 2,500 (M)
Total Fat	3 g	60 g or less (F), 70 g or less (M)
Saturated fat	2 g	20 g or less (F), 23 g or less (M)
Cholesterol	10 mg	300 mg or less
Sodium	63 mg	2,400 mg or less
Carbohydrates	9 g	250 g or more
Protein	1 g	55 g to 90 g

NOTES

117

SPICED GINGERBREAD MEN

It wouldn't be Christmas without a few jolly gingerbread people on your cookie platter.

Prep time: 45 minutes plus chilling
Baking time: 8 to 10 minutes
per batch
⬤ *Degree of difficulty: moderate*
❄ *Can be frozen up to 3 months*

2¾ **cups all-purpose flour**
2 **teaspoons cinnamon**
1 **teaspoon ginger**
1 **teaspoon baking soda**
¼ **teaspoon nutmeg**
¼ **teaspoon cloves**
¼ **teaspoon salt**
¾ **cup butter** *or* **margarine**
½ **cup granulated sugar**
½ **cup unsulphured molasses**
1 **large egg, lightly beaten**
  Currants (optional)

1 Combine the flour, cinnamon, ginger, baking soda, nutmeg, cloves, and salt in a medium bowl. Heat the butter, sugar, and molasses in a medium saucepan over medium heat until butter is melted. Remove from heat. Pour the melted butter mixture into flour mixture and stir until evenly moistened. Add the egg and stir until smooth. Let stand 10 minutes.

2 Divide dough in half. While still warm, between 2 sheets of wax paper, roll each half of dough ⅛ inch thick. Refrigerate on cookie sheets at least 1 hour or overnight.

3 Preheat oven to 350°F. Grease 2 cookie sheets. Remove wax paper and cut dough with a floured 5-inch gingerbread man-shaped cookie cutter. Transfer cut-outs to prepared cookie sheets. Decorate with currants, if desired. Bake 8 to 10 minutes. Transfer the cookies to wire racks to cool completely. Reroll scraps and refrigerate; repeat cutting and baking.

PER COOKIE		DAILY GOAL
Calories	115	2,000 (F), 2,500 (M)
Total Fat	5 g	60 g or less (F), 70 g or less (M)
Saturated fat	3 g	20 g or less (F), 23 g or less (M)
Cholesterol	19 mg	300 mg or less
Sodium	114 mg	2,400 mg or less
Carbohydrates	16 g	250 g or more
Protein	1 g	55 g to 90 g

FINAL TOUCHES

• It's simple to make your favorite cut-out cookies into ornaments. With the opening of a plain pastry tip, punch a small hole in the top of your favorite cut-out cookie and bake as directed. Decorate the cookie, then thread decorative ribbon through the hole and hang it from the Christmas tree.

• If you want to jazz up your cookies with delicious decorations, simply spread the cookies with a thin layer of Confectioners' Icing and sprinkle with colored sugar, nonpareils, or multi-colored or chocolate sprinkles. Cinnamon red hots, miniature chocolate chips, currants, shredded coconut, candied cherries, and candy-coated chocolate pieces can also be pressed into the icing.

DANISH JODEKAGER

The secret ingredient in these Yuletide treats is cardamom—the quintessential Scandinavian spice.

Prep time: 1 hour plus chilling
Baking time: 8 to 9 minutes
*   per batch*
◐   *Degree of difficulty: moderate*
❋   *Can be frozen up to 1 month*

2½   **cups all-purpose flour**
1½   **teaspoons cardamom**
  1   **teaspoon baking powder**
 ¼   **teaspoon salt**
  1   **cup unsalted butter, softened**
        (no substitutions)
  1   **cup granulated sugar, divided**
  1   **large egg**
 ½   **cup blanched almonds, ground**
  1   **large egg white, lightly beaten**

1   Combine the flour, cardamom, baking powder, and salt in a medium bowl. Beat the butter and ¾ cup of the sugar in a large mixing bowl at medium speed until light. Beat in the egg until light and fluffy.

Gradually beat in the flour mixture at low speed until combined. Shape dough into a ball, then flatten into a disk. Wrap and refrigerate 4 hours or overnight.

2   Preheat oven to 375°F. Grease 2 cookie sheets. Combine the almonds and the remaining ¼ cup sugar in a small bowl. Divide dough into quarters. Between 2 sheets of lightly floured wax paper, roll one quarter of dough ⅛ inch thick (keep remaining dough refrigerated). Remove wax paper and cut with a floured 3-inch round or heart-shaped cookie cutter.

3   Arrange the cut-outs 1 inch apart on prepared cookie sheets. Brush the tops with beaten egg white and sprinkle each with almond-sugar mixture. Bake 8 to 9 minutes, until edges are golden. Transfer the cookies to wire racks to cool completely. Repeat process with remaining dough and almond-sugar mixture, rerolling scraps. Makes 3½ dozen.

PER COOKIE		DAILY GOAL
Calories	100	2,000 (F), 2,500 (M)
Total Fat	6 g	60 g or less (F), 70 g or less (M)
Saturated fat	3 g	20 g or less (F), 23 g or less (M)
Cholesterol	17 mg	300 mg or less
Sodium	29 mg	2,400 mg or less
Carbohydrates	11 g	250 g or more
Protein	1 g	55 g to 90 g

THE ROAD TO EASY ROLLING

• If the chilled dough is too firm to roll out, allow it to sit at room temperature for 5 to 10 minutes to soften slightly.

• If your dough becomes too soft during rolling, simply place it in the refrigerator or freezer until it is firm and manageable again.

• Roll the cookie dough between 2 sheets of lightly floured wax paper. Remove the top sheet. Cut the dough into desired shapes, then freeze them on the wax paper until firm. Transfer the chilled cut-outs to prepared cookie sheets.

• To cut cookies, use floured cookie cutters. Start at the edge of the rolled dough and work toward the center. Reroll any scraps if directed.

MAPLE COOKIES

Nothing but real maple syrup will do in these fabulous cut-out cookies. We found the recipe in the cookbook *A Taste of Quebec* by Julian Armstrong.

Prep time: 45 minutes plus chilling
Baking time: 8 to 10 minutes
*   per batch*
Degree of difficulty: moderate
Can be frozen up to 3 months

3½ cups all-purpose flour
 2 teaspoons baking powder
 ½ teaspoon salt
 1 cup butter, softened
        (no substitutions)
 1 cup firmly packed brown sugar
 2 large eggs
 ⅓ cup pure maple syrup
 1 teaspoon vanilla extract
        Confectioners' Icing (recipe
            page 114)

1 Combine the flour, baking powder, and salt in a medium bowl. Beat the butter and brown sugar in a large mixing bowl at medium speed until light. Add the eggs, one at a time, beating until light and fluffy. Beat in the syrup and vanilla. Gradually beat in flour mixture at low speed just until combined. Divide dough into quarters. Wrap dough and refrigerate 4 hours or overnight.

2 Preheat oven to 350°F. Grease 2 cookie sheets. Between 2 sheets of wax paper, roll one quarter of dough ⅛ inch thick (keep remaining dough refrigerated). Remove top sheet of wax paper. Cut with floured cookie cutters into desired shapes.

3 Transfer cut-outs to prepared cookie sheets. Bake 8 to 10 minutes, until edges are golden. Transfer the cookies to wire racks to cool completely. Repeat rolling and cutting remaining dough, rerolling scraps. Decorate with Confectioners' Icing as desired. Makes 6 dozen.

PER COOKIE		DAILY GOAL
Calories	65	2,000 (F), 2,500 (M)
Total Fat	3 g	60 g or less (F), 70 g or less (M)
Saturated fat	2 g	20 g or less (F), 23 g or less (M)
Cholesterol	13 mg	300 mg or less
Sodium	57 mg	2,400 mg or less
Carbohydrates	9 g	250 g or more
Protein	1 g	55 g to 90 g

NOTES

COOKIE

DAZZLERS

Delight your holiday guests with this collection of party-perfect goodies. These cookies need only a dusting of sugar or a dip in chocolate to be absolutely spectacular. You'll get rave reviews when your dessert table includes elegant treats such as Linzer Spirals, piped Batons À L'Orange, or whipped-cream-filled Classic Brandy Snaps.

ESPRESSO STRIPS

These tender butter cookies are packed with rich coffee flavor thanks to instant espresso powder. For an extra fancy touch, dip the ends of the cookies in melted semisweet chocolate and chopped nuts.

Prep time: 35 minutes
Baking time: 12 to 14 minutes
  per batch
◑ *Degree of difficulty: moderate*
❄ *Can be frozen up to 1 month*

2½   cups all-purpose flour
     Pinch salt
1¼   **cups butter, softened**
        (no substitutions)
1   **cup granulated sugar**
2   **large egg yolks**
1   **tablespoon instant espresso powder**
1   **teaspoon vanilla extract**

1 Preheat oven to 350°F. Combine the flour and salt in a medium bowl. Beat the butter and sugar in a large mixing bowl at medium speed until light and fluffy. Beat in the egg yolks. Dissolve the espresso powder in the vanilla and add the mixture to the beaten butter-sugar mixture. Beat in flour mixture at low speed until combined.

2 Fit a large pastry bag with a ½-inch star tip. Fill with dough. Press 3-inch-long strips 2 inches apart onto ungreased cookie sheets. Bake 12 to 14 minutes, until edges are golden. Transfer the cookies to wire racks to cool completely . Makes 7 dozen.

PER COOKIE		DAILY GOAL
Calories	50	2,000 (F), 2,500 (M)
Total Fat	3 g	60 g or less (F), 70 g or less (M)
Saturated fat	2 g	20 g or less (F), 23 g or less (M)
Cholesterol	12 mg	300 mg or less
Sodium	30 mg	2,400 mg or less
Carbohydrates	5 g	250 g or more
Protein	.5 g	55 g to 90 g

CLASSIC BRANDY SNAPS

Imported golden syrup, available in many gourmet specialty markets, gives these delicate, extra-fancy cookies a rich toasty flavor. You'll love the contrast of the crisp cookie and velvety whipped cream filling.

Prep time: 25 minutes
Baking time: 7 to 10 minutes
*   per batch*
Degree of difficulty: moderate

½ **cup butter (no substitutions)**
½ **cup golden syrup (*or* 6 tablespoons**
    corn syrup and 2 tablespoons
    light molasses)
3 **tablespoons granulated sugar**
1 **teaspoon ginger**
    Pinch salt
1 **tablespoon brandy**
⅔ **cup all-purpose flour**
1½ **cups heavy *or* whipping cream**

1 Preheat oven to 350°F. Grease 2 cookie sheets. Bring butter, syrup, sugar, ginger, and salt to a boil in a heavy saucepan over medium heat. Remove from heat and stir in the brandy. Sift in the flour and whisk until smooth. Place the saucepan in a larger pan of hot water to keep the batter warm.

2 Drop batter by tablespoonfuls onto prepared cookie sheets (4 per sheet). Bake 7 to 10 minutes, until brown. Cool the cookies on cookie sheet 1 minute or just until they can be lifted without wrinkling but are still pliable. Invert the cookies onto the counter and roll them around a broom handle or cannoli mold, pressing to seal the seam. (If the cookies harden before rolling, return them to oven 30 seconds to soften.) Transfer the cookies to wire racks to cool completely. Repeat with remaining batter. (Can be made ahead. Store in an airtight container at room temperature up to 2 days.)

3 Just before serving, beat the heavy cream in a large mixing bowl until stiff. Fill a large pastry bag fitted with a ½-inch star tip with whipped cream and pipe the cream into the centers of cookies. Makes 2 dozen.

PER COOKIE		DAILY GOAL
Calories	130	2,000 (F), 2,500 (M)
Total Fat	10 g	60 g or less (F), 70 g or less (M)
Saturated fat	6 g	20 g or less (F), 23 g or less (M)
Cholesterol	31 mg	300 mg or less
Sodium	61 mg	2,400 mg or less
Carbohydrates	10 g	250 g or more
Protein	1 g	55 g to 90 g

NOTES

SARAH BERNHARDTS

These indulgent confections are a triple treat—a chocolate ganache filling nestled on a crisp macaroon cookie dipped in melted chocolate. For an extravagant touch, decorate each of these gems with edible gold leaf. *Also pictured on page 122.*

Prep time: 1 hour plus chilling
Baking time: 10 to 12 minutes
per batch
◒ *Degree of difficulty: moderate*
❋ *Can be frozen up to 3 months*

1 **tube (7 ounces) *or* 1 can (8 ounces) almond paste**
½ **cup granulated sugar**
2 **large egg whites**
¼ **teaspoon almond extract**
 Pinch salt
¾ **cup heavy *or* whipping cream**
16 **squares (16 ounces) semisweet chocolate, chopped, divided**
2 **tablespoons unsalted butter (no substitutions)**
1 **teaspoon dark rum**
1 **tablespoon vegetable shortening**
 Edible gold leaf* (optional)

1 Preheat oven to 350°F. Line 3 cookie sheets with foil; set aside. Fit a large pastry bag with a ¼-inch plain tip. Combine the almond paste, sugar, egg whites, almond extract, and salt in a large mixing bowl. Beat at medium speed until smooth; increase speed to high and beat 2 minutes. Spoon the batter into the pastry bag and pipe ¾-inch rounds on prepared cookie sheets. Bake 10 to 12 minutes, until light golden. Cool completely on the cookie sheets on wire racks. Carefully peel the cookies from foil and set aside.

2 Meanwhile, for filling, heat the cream in a medium saucepan to just boiling. Remove from heat. Add 8 squares (8 ounces) of the chocolate, butter, and rum and stir until smooth. Let stand, stirring occasionally, until thick enough to pipe, about 40 minutes.

3 Fit pastry bag with a ½-inch plain tip. Spoon in the filling and pipe a small mound on the flat side of each macaroon. Place the macaroons on cookie sheets and refrigerate about 1 hour, until firm.

4 Melt the remaining 8 squares (8 ounces) chocolate and the shortening in a double boiler over hot, not boiling water, stirring until smooth; keep warm.

5 Dip 1 cookie, filling side down, in chocolate to coat, then place the cookie chocolate side up on a jelly-roll pan. Repeat with remaining cookies. Refrigerate until firm. Decorate each cookie with a small piece of gold leaf, if desired. Makes 8 dozen.

PER COOKIE		DAILY GOAL
Calories	55	2,000 (F), 2,500 (M)
Total Fat	3 g	60 g or less (F), 70 g or less (M)
Saturated fat	2 g	20 g or less (F), 23 g or less (M)
Cholesterol	21 mg	300 mg or less
Sodium	32 mg	2,400 mg or less
Carbohydrates	5 g	250 g or more
Protein	0 g	55 g to 90 g

NOTES

MOCHA-ALMOND SANDWICHES

Filled with creamy semisweet chocolate, the toasted almonds give the espresso-flavored meringues extra crunch.

Prep time: 30 minutes plus cooling
Baking time: 1 hour 15 minutes
O *Degree of difficulty: easy*

½ **cup blanched slivered almonds**
2 **large egg whites, at room temperature**
¼ **teaspoon cream of tartar**
⅛ **teaspoon salt**
½ **cup granulated sugar**
½ **teaspoon vanilla extract**
2 **teaspoons instant espresso powder**
4 **squares (4 ounces) semisweet chocolate, coarsely chopped**
Unsweetened cocoa powder, for garnish

1 Preheat oven to 350°F. Spread the almonds on a baking sheet in a single layer. Bake 8 to 10 minutes, until lightly browned and fragrant. Cool completely then finely chop. Reduce oven temperature to 225°F. Line 2 cookie sheets with foil.

2 Beat the egg whites in a large mixing bowl at medium speed until foamy. Add the cream of tartar and salt and continue to beat until soft peaks form. Gradually beat in the sugar, one tablespoon at a time, then continue to beat until stiff. Beat in the vanilla. Gently fold the almonds and espresso powder into whites with a rubber spatula just until blended.

3 Spoon the meringue into a large pastry bag fitted with a ¾-inch plain tip. Pipe into 2-inch circles onto prepared cookie sheets. Bake 1 hour 15 minutes. Turn oven off. Cool in oven at least 1½ hours or overnight.

4 Melt the chocolate in the top of a double boiler over simmering water. Carefully peel the meringues from foil. Spread the flat side of half the meringues with some of the melted chocolate. Top with remaining meringues. Sift the cocoa over the tops of the cookies and drizzle them with remaining chocolate. Transfer the cookies to wire racks and let stand until chocolate is set. Makes 1½ dozen.

PER COOKIE		DAILY GOAL
Calories	75	2,000 (F), 2,500 (M)
Total Fat	4 g	60 g or less (F), 70 g or less (M)
Saturated fat	1 g	20 g or less (F), 23 g or less (M)
Cholesterol	0 mg	300 mg or less
Sodium	23 mg	2,400 mg or less
Carbohydrates	10 g	250 g or more
Protein	1 g	55 g to 90 g

NOTES

LEMON TASSIES

These miniature lemon pies come, from the Winston-Salem Community Cookbook, "Heritage of Hospitality." With a dollop of whipped cream, each one is a beauty.

Prep time: 25 minutes
Baking time: 40 to 45 minutes
Degree of difficulty: easy

½ cup butter, softened
    (no substitutions)
1 package (3 ounces) cream cheese,
    softened
1¼ cups all-purpose flour
⅔ cup granulated sugar
2 large eggs
3 tablespoons fresh lemon juice
3 tablespoons butter, melted
    Whipped cream, for garnish

1 Beat the softened butter and cream cheese in a large mixing bowl at medium speed until light and fluffy. Add flour and beat until crumbly. Lightly knead dough until it holds together and shape into a ball.

2 Preheat oven to 350°F. Spray 1¾-inch miniature muffin pan cups with vegetable cooking spray. Pinch the pastry off 1 tablespoon at a time and press into prepared muffin cups.

3 Mix the sugar, eggs, lemon juice, and melted butter in a medium bowl. Divide the filling evenly among muffin cups. Bake 40 to 45 minutes. Remove cookies from pans while slightly warm and transfer them to wire racks to cool completely. Top each tassie with a dollop of whipped cream. Makes 20.

PER COOKIE WITHOUT WHIPPED CREAM		DAILY GOAL
Calories	135	2,000 (F), 2,500 (M)
Total Fat	8 g	60 g or less (F), 70 g or less (M)
Saturated fat	5 g	20 g or less (F), 23 g or less (M)
Cholesterol	43 mg	300 mg or less
Sodium	83 mg	2,400 mg or less
Carbohydrates	13 g	250 g or more
Protein	2 g	55 g to 90 g

PALMIERS

Preparing puff pastry is easier than you think. If you make sure your dough is always thoroughly chilled while you're working with it, you'll create the flakiest cookie ever.

Prep time: 40 minutes plus chilling
Baking time: 20 minutes per batch
Degree of difficulty: moderate
Can be frozen up to 3 months

1½ **cups all-purpose flour**
⅛ **teaspoon salt**
1 **cup cold unsalted butter**
  (no substitutions), cut up
½ **cup sour cream**
  Granulated sugar

1 Combine the flour and salt in a large bowl. Cut in the butter with a pastry blender or 2 knives until mixture resembles coarse crumbs. Stir in the sour cream. Turn dough out onto a smooth surface and knead 6 to 8 times, until mixture holds together. Shape into a ball, then flatten slightly into a disk and wrap well in plastic wrap. Refrigerate overnight.

2 Unwrap chilled dough and cut into 4 equal pieces. Work with 1 piece at a time (keep remaining dough refrigerated). Sprinkle 2 tablespoons sugar on a 15-inch sheet of wax paper and roll the dough, rotating and turning often, into a 12x5-inch rectangle. Remove wax paper. With a small sharp knife, lightly mark the halfway point of the 12-inch side. Roll both 5-inch sides jelly-roll fashion toward center until they just meet. Wrap well and freeze 30 minutes or refrigerate overnight. Repeat rolling and chilling with remaining dough.

3 Line 2 cookie sheets with parchment paper. Place ¼ cup sugar on a sheet of wax paper. Cut each roll into ½-inch-thick slices, then dip each cut side into sugar. Place cut side down on prepared cookie sheets 2½ inches apart. Return the cookies to freezer until firm.

4 Adust oven rack to top position. Preheat oven to 375°F. Bake 15 minutes, until golden around edges. Turn the cookies over and bake 5 minutes more. Transfer the cookies to wire racks to cool completely. Makes 3 dozen.

PER COOKIE		DAILY GOAL
Calories	75	2,000 (F), 2,500 (M)
Total Fat	6 g	60 g or less (F), 70 g or less (M)
Saturated fat	4 g	20 g or less (F), 23 g or less (M)
Cholesterol	15 mg	300 mg or less
Sodium	10 mg	2,400 mg or less
Carbohydrates	5 g	250 g or more
Protein	1 g	55 g to 90 g

NOTES

131

MAIDS OF HONOR

Traditionally, this elegant cookie is served as part of an English tea, but we love these dainty almond tartlets with a bowl of fresh raspberries and whipped cream.

Prep time: 30 minutes plus chilling
Baking time: 20 to 22 minutes
● *Degree of difficulty: moderate*
❋ *Can be frozen up to 1 month*

¾ **cup all-purpose flour**
1 **tablespoon plus 1 teaspoon granulated sugar, divided**
⅛ **teaspoon salt**
3 **tablespoons cold butter, cut up (no substitutions)**
1 **tablespoon cold vegetable shortening**
2 **to 3 tablespoons ice water**
½ **cup almond paste**
1 **large egg**
3 **tablespoons heavy *or* whipping cream**
1 **teaspoon grated lemon peel**

1 Combine the flour, 1 teaspoon of the sugar, and salt in a medium bowl. With pastry blender or 2 knives, cut in the butter and shortening until mixture resembles coarse crumbs. Add ice water, one tablespoon at a time, tossing with a fork until mixture is moist enough to hold together. Wrap and refrigerate 30 minutes.

2 On a lightly floured surface, roll pastry ⅛ inch thick. Line fifteen 2-inch round tartlet molds with the pastry. Reroll scraps and line 15 more molds. Place the pastry-lined molds on 2 cookie sheets. Refrigerate while preparing filling.

3 Preheat oven to 400°F. Beat the almond paste and the remaining tablespoon of sugar in a large mixing bowl at medium speed until combined. Add the egg and beat until light and fluffy. Stir in the cream and lemon peel.

4 Spoon 1 teaspoon of the filling into each pastry shell. Bake 20 to 22 minutes, until golden. Immediately remove tartlets from molds and transfer them to wire racks to cool completely. Makes 30.

PER COOKIE		DAILY GOAL
Calories	50	2,000 (F), 2,500 (M)
Total Fat	3 g	60 g or less (F), 70 g or less (M
Saturated fat	1 g	20 g or less (F), 23 g or less (M
Cholesterol	12 mg	300 mg or less
Sodium	24 mg	2,400 mg or less
Carbohydrates	5 g	250 g or more
Protein	1 g	55 g to 90 g

NOTES

CRANBERRY HEARTS

These cookies with bright red cranberry centers are the perfect way to say "I love you."

Prep time: 1 hour plus chilling
Baking time: 12 to 15 minutes per batch
Degree of difficulty: moderate
Can be frozen up to 1 month

½ cups all-purpose flour
¼ teaspoon salt
1 cup butter, softened
      (no substitutions)
½ cups granulated sugar, divided
1 large egg
1 teaspoon vanilla extract
⅓ cups cranberries
2 tablespoons water
      Confectioners' sugar, for garnish

Combine the flour and salt in a medium bowl. Beat the butter and 1 cup of the sugar in a large mixing bowl at medium speed until light and fluffy. Add the egg and vanilla and beat until blended. Beat in flour mixture at low speed just until combined. Divide dough into quarters. Wrap each piece and refrigerate 4 hours or overnight.

2 Grease 4 cookie sheets. Between 2 sheets of lightly floured wax paper, roll 1 dough quarter ⅛ inch thick (keep remaining dough refrigerated). Cut with a floured 3½-inch heart-shape cookie cutter. Transfer the cut-outs to prepared cookie sheets. Cut the centers of half the unbaked cookies with a 2-inch heart-shape cutter. Chill all heart cookies on cookie sheets until firm.

3 Meanwhile, heat the cranberries, the remaining ½ cup sugar, and water to boiling in a medium saucepan over medium heat. Simmer until berries pop, 3 minutes. Remove from heat and cool. Puree the filling in a blender until smooth.

4 Preheat oven to 350°F. Spoon 1 level measuring teaspoon of filling onto the center of each heart that does not have a cut-out and brush edges with water. Top each filled heart with 1 cut-out heart, pressing edges to seal. Bake 8 to 9 minutes, until edges are golden. Transfer the cookies to wire racks to cool completely. Dust the tops of cookies with confectioners' sugar. Makes 28.

PER COOKIE		DAILY GOAL
Calories	150	2,000 (F), 2,500 (M)
Total Fat	7 g	60 g or less (F), 70 g or less (M)
Saturated fat	4 g	20 g or less (F), 23 g or less (M)
Cholesterol	25 mg	300 mg or less
Sodium	95 mg	2,400 mg or less
Carbohydrates	20 g	250 g or more
Protein	1 g	55 g to 90 g

NOTES

BATONS À L'ORANGE

These elegant finger cookies can be prepared with a cookie press or a pastry bag. They freeze beautifully, but it's best to dip the ends in chocolate the day you plan to serve them.

> Prep time: 30 minutes
> Baking time: 10 to 12 minutes
>   per batch
> ● Degree of difficulty: moderate
> ❄ Can be frozen up to 1 month

2¼ cups all-purpose flour
1 teaspoon baking powder
1 cup butter, softened
    (no substitutions)
1 cup granulated sugar
1 large egg
1 teaspoon grated orange peel
4 squares (4 ounces) semisweet
    chocolate, chopped

1 Preheat oven to 350°F. Grease 2 cookie sheets. Combine the flour and baking powder in a medium bowl. Beat the butter and sugar in a large mixing bowl at medium speed until light and fluffy. Beat in the egg and orange peel. Beat in flour mixture at low speed just until combined.

2 Attach rosette tip to a cookie press or fit a large pastry bag with a large star tip. Fill with dough. Press 3-inch long strips 2 inches apart onto prepared cookie sheets. Bake 10 to 12 minutes, until edges are golden. Transfer to wire racks to cool completely.

3 Melt the chocolate in the top of a double boiler over hot, not boiling, water. Dip each end of cooled cookies into melted chocolate. Place cookies on wire racks until chocolate is set. Makes 4 dozen.

PER COOKIE		DAILY GOAL
Calories	85	2,000 (F), 2,500 (M)
Total Fat	5 g	60 g or less (F), 70 g or less (M)
Saturated fat	3 g	20 g or less (F), 23 g or less (M)
Cholesterol	15 mg	300 mg or less
Sodium	49 mg	2,400 mg or less
Carbohydrates	10 g	250 g or more
Protein	1 g	55 g to 90 g

CHECKERBOARDS

Kids will love assembling these icebox cookies. The sugar 'n' spice doughs bake up "checkerboard-style" like magic!

Prep time: 1 hour plus chilling
Baking time: 10 to 15 minutes
*   per batch*
◐ *Degree of difficulty: moderate*
❋ *Can be frozen up to 3 months*

Spice Dough
  2 **cups all-purpose flour**
  2 **teaspoons ginger**
1½ **teaspoons cinnamon**
 ½ **teaspoon baking powder**
 ½ **teaspoon salt**
 ¼ **teaspoon cloves**
 ¾ **cup butter, softened**
     (no substitutions)
 ¾ **cup firmly packed brown sugar**
  1 **large egg**

Sugar Dough
  2 **cups all-purpose flour**
 ½ **teaspoon baking powder**
 ½ **teaspoon salt**

 ¾ **cup butter, softened**
     (no substitutions)
 ¾ **cup granulated sugar**
  1 **large egg**
  1 **teaspoon vanilla extract**
  1 **large egg yolk, beaten**

1 For Spice Dough, combine the flour, ginger, cinnamon, baking powder, salt, and cloves in a medium bowl. Beat the butter and brown sugar in a large mixing bowl at medium speed until light and fluffy. Add the egg and beat well. Beat in flour mixture at low speed just until combined. Divide dough in quarters. Shape each quarter into an 8-inch log. Wrap in wax paper; flatten all sides to form square logs. Wrap and refrigerate overnight.

2 For Sugar Dough, combine the flour, baking powder, and salt in a medium bowl. Beat the butter and sugar in a clean mixing bowl at medium speed until light and fluffy. Beat in the egg and vanilla. Beat in flour mixture at low speed just until combined. Divide dough in quarters. Shape each quarter into an 8-inch log. Wrap in wax paper; flatten all sides to form square logs. Wrap and refrigerate overnight.

3 On a sheet of wax paper, brush the beaten egg yolk along 1 long side of the spice log. Attach the spice log to a long side of a sugar log. Brush the top with yolk. Repeat with another spice log and sugar log. Brush the top of one spice-sugar log with egg yolk. Stack the other spice-log and sugar log on top of it, alternating colors in a checkerboard pattern. Make another checkerboard with remaining 4 logs. Wrap and refrigerate until firm, 4 hours or overnight.

4 Preheat oven to 350°F. Grease 2 cookie sheets. Cut scant ¼-inch-thick slices from logs and place them on prepared cookie sheets. Bake 10 to 15 minutes, until tops are firm and edges are golden. Transfer the cookies to wire racks to cool completely. Makes 6 dozen.

PER COOKIE		DAILY GOAL
Calories	80	2,000 (F), 2,500 (M)
Total Fat	4 g	60 g or less (F), 70 g or less (M)
Saturated fat	2.5 g	20 g or less (F), 23 g or less (M)
Cholesterol	19 mg	300 mg or less
Sodium	80 mg	2,400 mg or less
Carbohydrates	10 g	250 g or more
Protein	1 g	55 g to 90 g

APRICOT-ALMOND CRESCENTS

We love these super flaky cookies filled with apricot purée and rolled in almond-sugar glaze. They come to us from The Heritage Cookbook, a community cookbook published in Salt Lake City, Utah.

Prep time: 1 hour plus chilling
Baking time: 15 minutes per batch
Degree of difficulty: moderate
Can be frozen up to 1 month

1   container (8 ounces) creamed
        (4% fat) cottage cheese
2   cups all-purpose flour
1   cup butter, cut up
        (no substitutions)
8   ounces dried apricots
2⅓ cups granulated sugar, divided
1½ cups almonds, ground
4   large egg whites, lightly beaten

1   Combine the cottage cheese and flour in a large bowl. With a pastry blender or 2 knives, cut in the butter until mixture resembles coarse crumbs. On a work surface, gently knead dough until it holds together. Shape into 1-inch balls and transfer to a jelly-roll pan. Cover and refrigerate overnight.

2   Place the apricots in a small saucepan and cover with water; bring to a boil. Reduce heat and simmer about 20 minutes, until tender. Drain and transfer the apricots to a food processor and purée until smooth. Transfer the purée to a bowl and stir in 1 cup of the sugar; cool completely.

3   Combine the almonds and the remaining 1⅓ cups sugar in a small bowl and set aside.

4   Preheat oven to 375°F. Grease 2 cookie sheets. On a lightly floured surface, roll each chilled ball of pastry into a 3-inch round. (Shape only 10 cookies at a time so the pastry will remain chilled.) Place 1 teaspoon of filling in the center of the round; roll up in the shape of a crescent. Brush the tops of the crescents with egg white, then roll them in almond-sugar mixture and arrange on prepared cookie sheets. Bake 15 minutes, until lightly browned. Sprinkle with more almond-sugar if desired. Transfer the cookies to wire racks to cool completely. Repeat process with remaining pastry, filling, and almond-sugar mixture. Makes 5 dozen.

PER COOKIE		DAILY GOAL
Calories	105	2,000 (F), 2,500 (M)
Total Fat	5 g	60 g or less (F), 70 g or less (M)
Saturated fat	2 g	20 g or less (F), 23 g or less (M)
Cholesterol	9 mg	300 mg or less
Sodium	52 mg	2,400 mg or less
Carbohydrates	14 g	250 g or more
Protein	2 g	55 g to 90 g

NOTES

137

FILBERT DIAMONDS

Ultra-thin, these flourless hazelnut cookies are luscious plain or dipped in chocolate.

Prep time: 45 minutes plus chilling
Baking time: 10 minutes per batch
⬤ *Degree of difficulty: moderate*
❊ *Can be frozen up to 3 months*

1½ **cups plus 36 hazelnuts**
4 **large egg yolks**
1 **cup granulated sugar, divided**
3 **squares (3 ounces) semisweet
    chocolate, coarsely chopped**

1 Preheat oven to 350°F. Spread the hazelnuts on a baking sheet in a single layer. Bake 12 to 15 minutes, until lightly browned and skins are crackly. Wrap nuts in a clean kitchen towel and let stand 5 minutes. Rub the nuts in the towel to remove skins, then cool completely. Set aside 36 whole hazelnuts and cut them in half for garnish.

2 Beat the egg yolks with ¾ cup of the sugar in a large mixing bowl at medium-high speed until light and fluffy. Place the 1½ cups hazelnuts and the remaining ¼ cup sugar in a food processor and process until finely ground. Stir the ground nuts into the egg mixture until blended. Wrap and refrigerate dough 4 hours or overnight.

3 Preheat oven to 350°F. Lightly grease a cookie sheet. Divide dough in half. Roll one half of dough ⅛ inch thick between 2 sheets of wax paper (keep remaining dough refrigerated). Remove top sheet of wax paper and invert the dough onto a prepared cookie sheet. Remove second sheet of wax paper. Cut dough into 2-inch-wide strips, then diagonally at 2-inch intervals to form diamonds. Top each diamond with a hazelnut half.

4 Bake 10 minutes. Immediately recut the cookies and separate them. Transfer the cookies to wire racks to cool completely. Repeat process with remaining dough and scraps.

5 Melt the chocolate in a double boiler over hot, not boiling, water until smooth. Remove from heat and cool slightly. Dip an edge of cooled cookies in melted chocolate. Makes 6 dozen.

PER COOKIE		DAILY GOAL
Calories	45	2,000 (F), 2,500 (M)
Total Fat	3 g	60 g or less (F), 70 g or less (M)
Saturated fat	0 g	20 g or less (F), 23 g or less (M)
Cholesterol	12 mg	300 mg or less
Sodium	1 mg	2,400 mg or less
Carbohydrates	4 g	250 g or more
Protein	1 g	55 g to 90 g

NOTES

VIENNESE NUT CRESCENTS

These elegant Austrian sandwich cookies, filled with apricot jam, are very delicate, so if you make them ahead, fill just before serving.

Prep time: 30 minutes
Baking time: 15 minutes per batch
Degree of difficulty: moderate
Can be frozen up to 1 month

1¼ **cups hazelnuts**
⅓ **cup granulated sugar**
¼ **cup all-purpose flour**
   Pinch salt
3 **large egg whites, at room temperature**
2 **tablespoons butter, melted and cooled (no substitutions)**
¼ **cup apricot jam**
   Confectioners' sugar

1 Preheat oven to 350°F. Spread the hazelnuts on a baking sheet in a single layer. Bake 12 to 15 minutes, until lightly browned and skins are crackly. Wrap nuts in a clean kitchen towel and let stand 5 minutes. Rub the nuts in the towel to remove skins, then cool completely. Leave oven on.

2 Grease 2 cookie sheets. Place the hazelnuts and sugar in a food processor and process until finely ground. Add the flour and salt; pulse to combine. Beat the egg whites in a large mixing bowl at medium-high speed until stiff but not dry. Gently fold in the nut mixture, then the melted butter.

3 Spoon the batter into a large pastry bag fitted with a ⅜-inch round tip. Pipe 2-inch crescents on prepared cookie sheets. Bake 15 minutes, until firm. Transfer the cookies to wire racks to cool completely. Just before serving, spread apricot jam on the flat sides of half the cookies and top with the remaining cookies. Sprinkle with confectioners' sugar. Makes 2 dozen.

PER COOKIE		DAILY GOAL
Calories	75	2,000 (F), 2,500 (M)
Total Fat	5 g	60 g or less (F), 70 g or less (M)
Saturated fat	1 g	20 g or less (F), 23 g or less (M)
Cholesterol	3 mg	300 mg or less
Sodium	26 mg	2,400 mg or less
Carbohydrates	7 g	250 g or more
Protein	1 g	55 g to 90 g

NOTES

LINZER SPIRALS

These are not your ordinary slice-and-bake cookies, and after one bite you'll know why. The classic flavor combo of toasted hazelnuts and raspberries have made these crisp morsels one of our favorites.

Prep time: 35 minutes plus chilling
Baking time: 6 to 7 minutes per batch
Degree of difficulty: moderate
Can be frozen up to 3 months

⅓ **cup hazelnuts**
1½ **cups all-purpose flour**
½ **teaspoon baking soda**
⅛ **teaspoon cardamom**
  Pinch salt
½ **cup butter, softened**
    (no substitutions)
½ **cup granulated sugar**
1 **large egg**
½ **cup seedless raspberry preserves**

1 Preheat oven to 350°F. Spread the hazelnuts on a baking sheet in a single layer. Bake 12 to 15 minutes, until lightly browned and skins are crackly. Wrap nuts in a clean kitchen towel and let stand

5 minutes. Rub the nuts in the towel to remove skins, then cool completely. Place nuts in a food processor and process until finely ground.

2 Combine the nuts, flour, baking soda, cardamom, and salt in a medium bowl. Beat the butter and sugar in a large mixing bowl at medium speed until light and fluffy. Add the egg and beat well. Beat in flour mixture at low speed just until combined.

3 Divide dough in half. Roll each half between 2 sheets of wax paper into a 10x7-inch rectangle. Place on a cookie sheet and refrigerate until just firm, 10 to 15 minutes.

4 Remove the top sheet from one rectangle and spread half the preserves evenly over dough, leaving a ¼-inch border. Using wax paper as a guide, roll the dough up from one long edge, jelly-roll fashion. (If the dough cracks, let it stand at room temperature 5 minutes.) Repeat with remaining dough and preserves. Wrap rolls in wax paper and freeze 1 hour or refrigerate overnight.

5 Preheat oven to 350°F. Grease 2 cookie sheets. Slice rolls a scant ¼ inch thick. Place slices on prepared cookie sheets 2 inches apart. Bake 6 to 7 minutes, until edges are golden. Transfer the cookies to wire racks to cool completely. Makes 5½ dozen.

PER COOKIE		DAILY GOAL
Calories	40	2,000 (F), 2,500 (M)
Total Fat	2 g	60 g or less (F), 70 g or less (M)
Saturated fat	1 g	20 g or less (F), 23 g or less (M)
Cholesterol	7 mg	300 mg or less
Sodium	29 mg	2,400 mg or less
Carbohydrates	5 g	250 g or more
Protein	0 g	55 g to 90 g

NOTES

METRIC COOKING HINTS

By making a few conversions, cooks in Australia, Canada, and the United Kingdom can use the recipes in Ladies' *Home Journal® 100 Great Cookie Recipes* with confidence. The charts on this page provide a guide for converting measurements from the U.S. customary system, which is used throughout this book, to the imperial and metric systems. There also is a conversion table for oven temperatures to accommodate the differences in oven calibrations.

Volume and Weight: Americans traditionally use cup measures for liquid and solid ingredients. The chart (top right) shows the approximate imperial and metric equivalents. If you are accustomed to weighing solid ingredients, here are some helpful approximate equivalents.
■ 1 cup butter, castor sugar, or rice = 8 ounces = about 250 grams
■ 1 cup flour = 4 ounces = about 125 grams
■ 1 cup icing sugar = 5 ounces = about 150 grams
  Spoon measures are used for smaller amounts of ingredients. Although the size of the tablespoon varies slightly among countries, for practical purposes and for recipes in this book, a straight substitution is all that's necessary.
  Measurements made using cups or spoons should always be level, unless stated otherwise.

Product Differences: Most of the ingredients called for in the recipes in this book are available in English-speaking countries. However, some are known by different names. Here are some common American ingredients and their possible counterparts:
■ Sugar is granulated or castor sugar.
■ Powdered sugar is icing sugar.
■ All-purpose flour is plain household flour or white flour. When self-rising flour is used in place of all-purpose flour in a recipe that calls for leavening, omit the leavening agent (baking soda or baking powder) and salt.
■ Light corn syrup is golden syrup.
■ Cornstarch is cornflour.
■ Baking soda is bicarbonate of soda.
■ Vanilla is vanilla essence.

USEFUL EQUIVALENTS

⅛ teaspoon = 0.5 ml
¼ teaspoon = 1 ml
½ teaspoon = 2 ml
1 teaspoon = 5 ml
¼ cup = 2 fluid ounces = 50 ml
⅓ cup = 3 fluid ounces = 75 ml
½ cup = 4 fluid ounces = 125 ml

⅔ cup = 5 fluid ounces = 150 ml
¾ cup = 6 fluid ounces = 175 ml
1 cup = 8 fluid ounces = 250 ml
2 cups = 1 pint
2 pints = 1 litre
½ inch = 1 centimetre
1 inch = 2 centimetres

BAKING PAN SIZES

American	Metric
8x1½-inch round baking pan	20x4-centimetre sandwich or cake tin
9x1½-inch round baking pan	23x3.5-centimetre sandwich or cake tin
11x7x1½-inch baking pan	28x18x4-centimetre baking pan
13x9x2-inch baking pan	32.5x23x5-centimetre baking pan
2-quart rectangular baking dish	30x19x5-centimetre baking pan
15x10x2-inch baking pan	38x25.5x2.5-centimetre baking pan (Swiss roll tin)
9-inch pie plate	22x4- or 23x4-centimetre pie plate
7- or 8-inch springform pan	18- or 20-centimetre springform or loose-bottom cake tin
9x5x3-inch loaf pan	23x13x6-centimetre or 2-pound narrow loaf pan or paté tin
1½-quart casserole	1.5-litre casserole
2-quart casserole	2-litre casserole

OVEN TEMPERATURE EQUIVALENTS

Fahrenheit Setting	Celsius Setting*	Gas Setting
300°F	150°C	Gas Mark 2
325°F	160°C	Gas Mark 3
350°F	180°C	Gas Mark 4
375°F	190°C	Gas Mark 5
400°F	200°C	Gas Mark 6
425°F	220°C	Gas Mark 7
450°F	230°C	Gas Mark 8
Broil		Grill

Electric and gas ovens may be calibrated using Celsius. However, increase the Celsius setting 10 to 20 degrees when cooking above 160°C with an electric oven. For convection or forced-air ovens (gas or electric), lower the temperature setting 10°C when cooking at all heat levels.